No More Strangers

Now therefore ye are no more strangers and foreigners, but fellowcitizens with the saints, and of the household of God;

And are built upon the foundation of the apostles and prophets, Jesus Christ himself being the chief corner stone. (Ephesians 2:19-20.)

No More Strangers

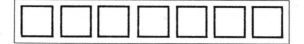

HARTMAN AND CONNIE RECTOR

BOOKCRAFT INC.
SALT LAKE CITY, UTAH

1971

13th Printing, 1975

LITHOGRAPHED IN U S A BY

PUBLISHERS PRESS
SALT LAKE CITY, UTAH

CONTENTS

PREFACE

The convert's story is dear to our hearts. We came in from the outside. We retain vivid recollections of what life was like without the gospel, of the anxious search, and of what it was like to step from darkness into light.

The conversion story is in a sense an integral part of every Church member's life, since all of us at some point owe our membership to missionary endeavor, formal or otherwise. No doubt this is one reason why the outstanding stories of conversion in the early Church have had such a great appeal. For the same reason, well-told modern accounts of conversions to the gospel touch the heart and thrill the soul.

Every true conversion to the gospel involves a miracle — the transformation of a life. Some display in addition the interest of special features, unusual circumstances, rare insights, and spiritual experiences. Such conversions are no more uncommon today than in any gospel dispensation, since they are prompted by the same Spirit. It is a selection of these conversion experiences which comprises this book.

Conversions seem to have one or a combination of four themes running as a thread through the fabric of the convert's testimony. Converts are profoundly impressed with:

1. The Church membership. A convert's association with the Latter-day Saint people in which he feels their true love and concern is often a new and inspiring experience.

2. The Book of Mormon. Many converts feel that this is the key to their conversion. Often they say, "I read the Book of Mormon and I *knew* it was true."

3. Prayer. Many converts confess that they had never prayed in their lives before being introduced to the restored gospel, even though they had been members of

a church all their lives. When they finally went upon their knees to the Lord in humble, sincere prayer, then they knew the gospel is true.

4. The missionaries. Many converts are tremendously impressed with the young men or women who come to them in the name of the Lord. They are amazed at their wisdom and the authority with which they speak. It is not uncommon to hear new converts say of the missionaries: "Their appearance was not striking, their diction and grammar were less than perfect, they did not possess great worldly knowledge, but there was just something about them that convinced me that what they were saying was true; in fact, I *knew* they were telling me the truth."

The book is frankly designed to promote the faith of the reader and to emphasize the great blessings which are available through the light of the gospel. Particularly impressive to us is the limitless potential for growth which the gospel offers. From our youth, we have felt the compelling urge to search for truth on the basis that we must never cease to grow. We bear personal witness that the mainstream of truth, the sublime opportunity for personal growth, is the gospel of Jesus Christ as taught by The Church of Jesus Christ of Latter-day Saints; that this gospel has been restored by heavenly beings to a prophet on earth after many centuries of apostasy; and that there is no other way to salvation.

Each of the contributors of this book bears a witness similar to ours. We are grateful to all of them for their willingness and wholehearted cooperation in permitting their stories to be published, and we join with them in expressing the hope that the book will be the means of building faith and conviction in all who read it.

We accept full responsibility for the compilation of this book. It is our own contribution and is in no way endorsed by the Church. Specifically, should any of the accounts be found to contain error, the Church and its leaders are completely absolved from responsibility for such error.

HARTMAN AND CONNIE RECTOR

HARTMAN RECTOR, JR.

MISSIONARIES FIND A
FUTURE GENERAL AUTHORITY

Hartman Rector is of that rare breed for whom the quest for truth has always been a compelling force. Born of honorable yet non-churchgoing parents, he early felt a keen need for the anchor of religious faith and works. But it had to be the true religion. He studied and prayed as his search intensified, but always something was lacking in the many churches he investigated.

Brother Rector's wife Connie was equally anxious for the right answers. The following account tells how those answers were supplied her, in her husband's absence from home, when two LDS missionaries knocked on the Rectors' door in San Diego in 1951. Neither the missionaries nor the Rectors could then have assessed the impact of that initial contact. Seventeen years later, Hartman Rector, Jr., was called to be a member of the First Council of Seventy.

From the period of my first recollection I had an almost insatiable desire to know the "truth."

As a small boy I tried to read the Bible, but I found it to be very difficult. I'm sure I never progressed beyond Genesis in the Old Testament, but I did read more of the New Testament. I can't remember anyone else in our home reading the scriptures, but my maternal grandmother had a big old picture Bible at her house. Once my appetite was whetted, I kept after her to read it to me. About three times each year I visited in her small home in Renick, Missouri. Many of my evenings there were spent on her lap. With her arms around me she would hold the Bible, and after reading the scriptures, she would give me her simplified interpretation.

The pictures in that old Bible were really wild. I remember being very frightened by the artist's conception of Abraham standing with a dagger over Isaac—a winged, feminine angel constraining Abraham by a gentle hand upon his arm. That picture also served to confirm my grandmother's firm belief that there were only female angels (no MAN deserved that exalted station)! As for me, I wondered where angels went when they "went up."

My grandmother warned me, "This old world is getting so bad that it is going to end!"

I'd say, "When's the end coming, Mama Garvin?"

"One of these days!" was always her answer, and I wanted to be among those who were pictured around Jesus instead of with the group who had fire and brimstone raining down upon them.

My family attended church only in the summertime. Each summer we attended four or five times (we didn't wear out the place). Stormy weather and the accompanying bad roads often kept us away; so did visiting cousins, or measles, or a baseball game—almost anything took precedence over church. Our biggest deterrent to attendance was my father's lack of conviction that there was any need for organized religion; as yet he has not joined a church. He purchased our first radio, a Zenith, with a wind-charger we mounted in the top of a tree. A sermon heard over this radio was usually quite enough religion each Sunday.

A revival week was held every summer in the small town where my grandmother lived, and I loved to attend these meetings with her. Those preachers could really build a fire under the local populace. They'd start preaching on Monday night, and along about Thursday they'd open the invitation to "accept Christ." The preacher made it sound so urgent, that I wanted to run forward and show my willingness to let Christ "take control" in my life so that I might "live for Jesus." I wasn't sure what that meant, but I wanted to do it anyway. However, Grandmother wouldn't let me go up and "confess."

"Your daddy might not want you to do that," she would say.

Once she agreed to speak to my mother when she came to take me home. My mother responded with, "Now you needn't worry about Junior; he is a good boy and will join the church when he is old enough to know what he is doing." Many of the other children with whom I played were allowed to join. I felt sure it would make a change in my life, but it was confusing to play later with some of the kids whom I had seen go up to "confess Christ." Some of the things we did didn't seem very Christlike, such as throwing mud clods at cars, and sticking potatoes on exhaust pipes, stealing bulbs out of taillights, etc.

During my childhood my father was an excellent example to me. He was as honest and honorable as any man I've ever known—completely just in his dealings with his fellowmen. I am convinced he would have walked ten miles to repay a debt of ten cents. If he gave his word, no written contract was necessary. He felt this was the only decent way to live. However, I must have wanted an outward sign, as a child. I was confused. If he was religious, why didn't we go to church? If he needed God, why didn't I see him pray? It seemed to me, also, that there was an occasional inconsistency in his actions; for instance, at one time he caught me smoking and gave me quite a thrashing, but he had to lay his own pipe down to do it.

I really didn't attend church regularly until I was serving in the Navy. We marched to divine services each Sunday evening in pre-flight training, and from that time on I attended regularly. Also, I read several books on religion and pondered a great deal on the subject.

The same contradiction or inconsistency I had felt at home seemed to run throughout this experience also—the difference between what is said and what is actually practiced. I noticed this in the churches whose doctrine I studied, for many times their tenets did not square with scripture. For me, there were too many questions left unanswered.

"If you can't explain it, then just believe it anyway," a minister once told me. "Faith requires you to do nothing; faith lets God do it all. Just have faith."

One time while going through the St. Louis railroad station, I met a minister at the servicemen's canteen. He invited me into a small conference room so that we could talk. He asked me if I belonged to a church; I replied that I did not. He said that in my career in the armed service I would, no doubt, find myself in company that would not be the best for me, that there would be girls who would desire my association and that my friends might try to convince me that it would be stupid not to take shrewd advantage of these situations. But he said that remaining clean and chaste was not stupid—it was very wise; and that although there were many who thought the life of Jesus Christ was a weak and senseless way to live, their opinion did not make it so. He said that a clean life was to be highly prized and that when I married—as I surely would some day—I should be as morally clean and virtuous as I would expect my bride to be. Living a pure life might be difficult but it would be well worth my efforts; for one thing, I would be better able to draw strength and courage to meet the challenge of demanding situations in the military. He also said it would be best for me to make my decision about this right then, while I could still view it with a detached perspective.

That encounter was very impressive to me. I knew that what he told me was true but I did not realize at that time that I had made a decision to follow his counsel. Afterwards I faced many dangerous moral situations, but somehow I came through unscathed, as though someone were protecting me.

The desire to know the truth was intensified as I studied and prayed and as I attended first one church and then another, but there was something missing in all of them for me. I formulated my own hodge-podge of a philosophy about life and death as I read numerous books and articles and listened to assorted sermons. But as I pondered the New Testament I found much that I could not understand. I decided that all religions were "man-made" and that therefore mine could be as valid as any other. My philosophy was that God does, in fact, exist, though what kind of a being he is I could not fathom. I believed that death was not the dreaded experience which everyone seemed to fear but that each individual did, in fact, go on living somewhere else, and also that rewards would be commensurate with works.

During Operational Training as a Navy aviator I attended a large Protestant church twice each Sunday and once during the week for the eight months of my stay in Jacksonville, Florida. I went there because I was sure the minister was going to give me the answers to my deepest questions. He was a tremendous preacher, and had one of the largest congregations in the city. I talked personally with him several times and he invited me to his home. I felt he came very close to answering my questions, but I was still dissatisfied.[1] The questions which most bothered me were:

1. Why did Jesus Christ have to be crucified?
2. How can his sacrifice really do something for me?
3. What can we expect after death?
4. Was there another life before mortality?
5. What is the real purpose of earth life?
6. How can one gain strength to live the "good life," or spiritual life, while living in a materialistic world?

There were other questions and irritations, and an undefined quest for just plain "truth" which I was reasonably sure I would recognize once I found it.

I was released from active duty in the Navy in 1947 and returned to my home in Missouri. There I married the beautiful little dark-haired girl I had met and briefly courted four years previously. I well remember the first time I saw her. She was walking down the street. I was eighteen and she was fourteen—and I knew immediately she was for me. I spoke to her that day and we got acquainted, and I later told her she had four years in which to "grow up" because I was going into the Navy but would come

---

[1]From a letter dated Feb. 14, 1947, NAS Charlestown, Rhode Island from Hartman Rector, Jr. to Connie Daniel (Rector):

"I stood on the corner at Five Points in Jacksonville last Tuesday night and wished very desperately that it was Sunday morning so I could walk in and hear Dr. Kissling deliver his usual very fine sermon. I know it would have been wonderful —I never heard one that wasn't—but I know also that I would come away with the feeling that there was still some little something lacking; there always was. I have no doubt that Dr. Kissling walks very near Him, maybe as near as man can walk to Him, but he is just on the other side of the oh-so-fine line that lets one in. I have never seen the face of the man that has been there. Why? Maybe because I am young—have not lived or looked long enough, or maybe it is because there are no such men. If that is true, again WHY? I think I shall always believe it is possible and I don't think I shall ever stop looking—I will give all, which in reality is nothing, for one moment when I know the truth."

back and marry her. I didn't know then how or why I knew her
but I know now. I'm sure we were very well acquainted before we
came to this earth. Marrying her was one of the most fortunate
things I have ever done, for, among other reasons, it was she who
was home when the missionaries came by and brought the truth
into our lives.

While we were still in our teens I told her that I wanted to
seek truth and we pledged together that we would continue to grow
in understanding and wisdom. I made the statement to her many
times in letters that "we must never cease to grow."[2]   I was
determined to keep growing, for I did not agree with Shakespeare's "from hour to hour, we ripe and ripe, and then, from
hour to hour, we rot and rot; and thereby hangs a tale."[3]   I could
not conceive of such a waste.

So, four years later I kept my promise and came back home
to court my sweetheart, and we were married about a year later.
After we were married we read and discussed the Bible together.
After the births of our first two children I was recalled with our
Naval aviators to participate in the Korean conflict. I was assigned
to a squadron based in San Diego, California, and then ordered
to Hawaii for thirteen weeks of special training. I left my little
family in San Diego.

No sooner had I departed and my wife had moved our
possessions into our rented home than the Mormon missionaries
came by and knocked on her door. They were using the poll
technique of tracting, and many of the questions on which they
"polled" her were the very questions we had pondered together,
so she was very interested.

In one of her letters to me she mentioned that two young men
had called on her and asked a lot of questions about religion, to
which they also then seemed to have all the answers. Well, that
made me a bit angry. What were young men doing calling on my

---

[2]From a letter dated Feb. 14, 1947, NAS Charlestown, Rhode Island from
Hartman Rector, Jr. to Connie Daniel (Rector):
". . . . and you will continue to grow; I know you will because I won't let you
stop, just as you won't let me stop—and God won't let either of us stop . . . it's
our only real duty, the only real duty of any and all men, and we won't shirk it . . .
through such growth is the only way we can come to understand God and his truth."
[3]From William Shakespeare's "As You Like It," act 2, scene 7.

wife, even in the name of a church, while I was away? I didn't like it, especially since *they* were answering questions that I had been trying to solve all my life.

When I returned home from Hawaii, on the first evening Connie, my wife, told me the Joseph Smith story. When she said that he had had visions and revelations it seemed so ridiculous that I laughed in her face, and this made her cry. I then saw how much the message really meant to her and I relented and said, "Well, the least I can do is read some of the material they left for you to study."

No sooner did I start to read the Book of Mormon than I knew that at last I had found that for which I had been searching.

While reading First Nephi, I remember saying to myself, "Dear God, let this be true, please let this be the truth—for if it is, it answers all the questions I have been trying to answer all my life." I hadn't finished Second Nephi when I knew it was true.

I had prayed one simple prayer to the Lord for many years: "Dear God, please show me the truth. Please lead me to the truth." I had sought truth in many places. Now here were two young men, Elders Teddy Raban and Ronald Flygare, boys really—their grammar was poor, their diction less than perfect, they had no great store of worldly knowledge—but they brought the truth right into my living room. And although they were very young, they had two great powers with them, truth and God. I could not argue against what they offered, neither did I wish to.

Not only did they bring me the truth, but they also insisted that I attend church. I could see no real necessity to go to church. I am sure my early training had left its mark and, too, I had not found church attendance particularly fruitful. Instead of providing answers in my quest, church attendance had placed me in contact with a group of people wanting to involve me in a lot of social activity. I often felt this was a waste of time since it provided no answers to questions of import.

However, because I trusted these young men, I agreed to go to church. My first church experience was in an investigators' class taught by a wonderful little man whose name was Joseph Smith

Wilson. Brother Wilson is a great authority on the Book of Mormon. He knows the book by page number. I would ask him questions and he would answer, "Brother Rector, the answer to that question is on page 104 of the Book of Mormon." Then he would read the answer. I would ask another question and he would respond, "That's on page 223." Then he would turn to page 223 and read the answer from the Book of Mormon.

I attended his class for only a few Sundays before it became time for me to leave for Korea. I thanked him for the time he had spent in answering my questions and told him I would probably not see him again for the next eight to ten months. He said, "Brother Rector, you will join the Church while you are away." I told him I didn't think I would because my wife and I wanted to join the Church together when we joined. He insisted that I would join the Church while I was away.

I went aboard ship on the last day of 1951 and took with me a triple combination (Book of Mormon, Doctrine and Covenants, and Pearl of Great Price) and *The Articles of Faith* by James E. Talmage. I read *The Articles of Faith* during the first month at sea. I enjoyed it so much that I wanted to read *Jesus the Christ*, another book by the same author. One evening in February I heard an announcement over the public address system aboard ship, that Latter-day Saint services would be held in the crew library at 7:30 p.m. At the appointed hour I went to the library where I found four young men who looked very much like the two young missionaries who had knocked upon my door in San Diego. I told them I was not a member of the Church but was interested in studying about it. They welcomed me with much enthusiasm and also with many answers to my questions. However, when I asked them for page numbers for their answers they were unable to accomodate me.

We then embarked on a very concentrated study of the gospel of Jesus Christ. While I was aboard ship I read fourteen of the best books that have ever been written. Included in this number were the standard works of the Church (Bible, Book of Mormon, Doctrine and Covenants, and Pearl of Great Price), also the writings of each of the presidents of the Church in this dispensation, plus the works of James E. Talmage and Orson Pratt and others. Such study was like food and drink to a starving man. I had searched for these answers for years, looked everywhere; and now at long last I was getting *all* my questions answered in full. I was ecstatic with joy and gratitude to my Father in heaven because of his great mercy to me.

When we arrived in Japan in the latter part of February 1952, the group decided that I was ready for baptism. So they accompanied me to the Japan Mission home where I announced to the mission president's counselor that I was ready for baptism. He eyed me very suspiciously and asked how long I had been investigating the Church. I told him, "Oh, four or five months I guess." He answered that I would need to investigate for at least one year before I could join. I insisted that I knew the gospel was true and was ready to join the Church. He then consented to interview me.

After an interview which took an hour and a half, I finally received a recommend for baptism. On February 25, 1952, in the garden behind the Japan Mission home in 30-degree weather, seven thousand miles from my home in Missouri, I was baptized. Later I was confirmed a member of The Church of Jesus Christ of Latter-day Saints. My search had come to an end.

My wife was baptized four days later in San Diego, California. We had agreed to write each other as we learned principles that were new to us. She would write to me and I would write to her, and many times our letters passed in the middle of the Pacific, each containing the same new principle. I was asking her if she could accept this doctrine and she was asking me if I could accept the same principle.

I am a witness before God that he lives and he hears and answers prayers, for he has heard and answered mine. I bear testimony that Jesus is the Christ, and that he lives; that he has re-established his true Church upon the earth in modern times through the Prophet Joseph Smith—great, great prophet that he was; and that the true Church of Jesus Christ is upon the earth today, presided over by a living prophet who has been chosen by the Lord for this particular purpose. These things I do not merely believe; I *know* with that sure witness which can come only from the Holy Ghost, through which all gospel truths can be known.

"Great is his [the Lord's] wisdom, marvelous are his ways, and the extent of his doings none can find out. His purposes fail not, neither are there any who can stay his hand. From eternity to eternity he is the same. . . ." (Doctrine and Covenants 76:2-4).

How gracious he is to those who diligently seek his face, for they shall find him and know that he is. To this I bear humble witness, in the name of Jesus Christ, my Redeemer, Amen.

NORMA RAMOS

THE GOAL OF ANGELS

When the gospel found Norma Ramos she was in the depths of sadness and bereft of hope for happiness. Born and raised in the small city of Cruz Alta, Brazil, she had enjoyed all the advantages of a fine intellect, a good education and a background of culture and refinement. Additionally she had been blessed with a high level of professional and material success. But she had watched this all slip from her grasp with the disintegration of her marriage, and she had returned with her children to struggle for a livelihood in her native city.

On a sad and boring Sunday afternoon, light streamed into the home with two young Americans. Only half in fun, she later called them the family's guardian angels. Hence the goal of angels which she set for her children.

Since her baptism, hope soars limitlessly and opportunities multiply. Her talents and experience are again used in larger fields of her country's service as well as in the Lord's kingdom. Small wonder that in gratitude, as she puts it, "my soul lives on its knees."

My family came from the north of Portugal and settled in Brazil two centuries ago. My great-grandfather was one of the founders of the city of Cruz Alta, my birthplace, although he never lived there. He purchased big areas of land, built houses, planted trees, and organized the ranch called Capão Ralo. This property has belonged to our family ever since then, and it is there where I lived the happiest days of my childhood and where I learned from my father to love nature.

I was educated in a practically non-religious home. My father, a reader of Renan and Voltaire, sometimes called himself a freethinker, but occasionally he admitted the existence of a Superior Power who rules the fate of man. My mother, who believed in spiritualism, did not practice religion.

When I was twelve, I entered a Methodist college, and there I learned much about Christianity. Several years later I married a young Catholic man and studied his Roman faith. He gave me books by Catholic writers, French writers mainly. And thus, seduced by the thoughts of Jacques Maritain, Mauriac Claudel, Leon Bloy, and others, I began to attend mass and was enchanted by the solemnity and formal beauty of the Latin worship in churches. I have always thought that unity of faith is necessary between a married couple; therefore, it was in the Catholic Church that we baptized the children, and I made a point to take them regularly to mass.

In those days I used to write tales and short novels, some of which were published in newspapers and literature magazines in Porto Alegre and Rio de Janeiro.

There was, however, in the deepest, most profound portion of my soul a great dissatisfaction—I was thirsty for the absolute. The replies to my questions were evasive almost in every case on the part of the churches I knew then.

We had moved to Bolivia where my husband became cultural attaché, and I myself was a professor of the Brazilian Cultural Center there. After going through many contrary times and distasteful events, I found there was no other alternative for me but to abandon that situation of material welfare and high social position and return to my small Cruz Alta, and thus seperate myself from my husband whom I considered lost from normal life. But I took with me the greatest treasure the Lord can give a woman in this world—my four little children, the oldest of whom was eleven and the youngest only four months.

Cruz Alta is a small city which offers extremely few opportunities for a woman who must struggle for a livelihood, and therefore, in spite of my being an educated member of one of the most traditional and esteemed families in the south country, I found myself facing serious problems. These I was finally able to overcome through my efforts for the sake of my children and with the help of my brother. I found two jobs: one as a teacher in the Normal School, and another as secretary to the Mayor; and later on, I became Director of the Museum. Through hard work, I was able to rent a big old house which offered relative comfort and dignity, and we moved into it. My children were growing up and apparently had forgotten the drama they had passed through. So we came to a point where we experienced no more grave problems; but neither did we have any great hopes.

One Sunday afternoon, after we had moved into this relatively comfortable old house, my children were playing in their rooms. I was alone with a feeling of great sadness, complete hopelessness, thinking my last opportunity for a bit of happiness had vanished forever, when I heard someone knocking at the door. I stood up and somewhat reluctantly went to see who it was. There stood the two young Americans whom I had observed in the neighborhood and about whom I had been very curious.

The first, who spoke timidly, asked me some questions which I answered somewhat jokingly; I was not exactly laughing at these young men, but I was amused at the sight of their extreme youth yet sober countenances. Then I became aware of the second missionary as he joined in the conversation, and although I did not know him, I had the strong impression of having recognized him, as though I were meeting an old friend again after a long absence. Our conversation that afternoon was the beginning of a great friendship.

To me, our conversation was a fine distraction for that boring Sunday afternoon, and I insisted on their coming in, but they declined my invitation and made an appointment instead for five o'clock the next afternoon. I awaited that visit like a girl awaiting a party, and ever after that I felt the same eagerness when the missionaries came to our home; they and their message were fascinating to me.

In the course of the first few visits, a pattern of discussion was established. I was reluctant to accept what they said and I jested with them; I did not like the manner they used to bring forth their subject and I tried to argue, but their dialectics were invincible. The philosophy they presented offered no weak points I eagerly read all booklets and publications they gave me. They asked me to pray also, but I used to forget, and each time they visited our home again I had to ashamedly confess that I had not done what I had promised.

Although at the beginning I did not take what they said very seriously, my attention was suddenly enlivened when they began to explain to me what the Book of Mormon was; and my interest turned into a passion for the book. Having lived seven years in Bolivia studying and observing the remains of the old Andean civilizations, I realized immediately the truth of the history I was being told, although some of the names which the elders mentioned, such as Nephi and Lehi, seemed fantastic to me. Up until then I had regarded Joseph Smith's story as nothing more than an absurd tale, although I did not feel that way about the ideas presented to me. From the very first day I felt the ideas and doctrines to be true; in fact, I *knew* them to be true. But the story about Joseph Smith seemed to me to be fictitious, and it was the part about his being a modern prophet that afflicted me the most. Nevertheless, knowing the truth of what the Book of Mormon contained, I realized that it could not possibly have been invented; that young, not-too-wise frontiersman could never have invented such a migration from Mesopotamia to America. Science has now found such an event to be evident, but in the time in which he lived it was considered nonsense. Also, the story of Lehi's family seemed to me much too beautiful not to be true.

I was greatly disturbed by my new knowledge, which accurately matched many facts with which I was acquainted but for which I had had no explanation until then. So I began to pray, longing to know whether or not the Book of Mormon was truly of God; and thus, I also had the pleasure of giving a positive answer to the anxious question the missionaries asked me every day: "Are you praying to know the truth?"

While I was discovering the doctrines of the Church of Jesus Christ, they entered into my heart and I realized that they were all true. In each case I found an answer to my old doubts, and all

I had instinctively felt was confirmed. This brought me great joy, but I also experienced great anguish. While I was with the missionaries I was extremely happy, as if I were in another world of perfection and purity; but after they were gone, I felt all the material foundations of my life being shaken by this new faith. My relatives did not at first regard my interest in the Church seriously, but later on I had to face their opposition and I finally lost the affection of a niece whom I loved dearly.

After much hesitation I accepted an invitation to go to the chapel, it was the Saturday before Easter when I went, and what a great disappointment it was! There was only one family there— very "ordinary" people—and they did everything. This family gave a presentation, and they themselves were the actors and the audience.

The next day, Easter Sunday, the missionaries accepted for the first time an invitation to have dinner at our home, and I challenged them then, asking them what kind of an undertaking that small church was. Where was the famous dynamic North American spirit, and after eight years of effort, where was the success? The young elder turned a good red (from anger, I think) and asked me what I, as a Brazilian, would suggest they should do to help the situation. This is exactly what I wanted. I offered to help them through articles in the local newspapers and broadcasting programs for the radio. Thus, before I was baptized I was working for the Church and cooperating with the missionaries. I had realized from the very beginning that this whole experience would be a call to serve others.

My heart was filled with joy and happiness for the knowledge I had acquired and for the many lights which were being turned on in my life, illuminating countless dark doubts which I possessed. I cannot say exactly when nor how it came to be, but my heart was flooded with an intense and profound love and gratitude, and these things transformed my life completely. I could find nothing within me to oppose the teachings I was being given, and from there on I understood and accepted everything as the truth.

My marriage had been destroyed by vice and intemperance, and I therefore accepted the Word of Wisdom as a blessing from heaven. Also I found in those two young men what I had been seeking since my separation from my husband; I found models for my children who had been left without a father. I kidded the missionaries and called them our guardian angels, and I instituted in our home a goal for which my children could strive: the goal of angels!

Now I was already working actively with the missionaries, writing a series of little articles in the newspaper under the title, "What Is a Mormon?" and also a radio program which was called "New Life." This was a precious opportunity to learn more of the doctrines and philosophy of the Church and also to collaborate with these extraordinary young persons.

One day as we were working on these articles, I asked, "Then how is this, you do not ask me to be baptized? Perhaps you do not want to baptize me under any circumstances?" It happened that because I had boldly declared to them that first day that I would never be baptized, since I had already been baptized, they had decided to wait until I myself should ask them to baptize me.

Thus the day was marked—Sunday, the 4th of May, 1969. The night before, the temperature fell terribly, and Sunday morning dawned very clear, full of sun, but with an icy south wind blowing—a sign of the beginning of winter.

My children and I traveled to the chapel with great anticipation. There, dressed in baptismal clothes and with a towel wrapped around me so I would feel a little less cold, I gave my first talk, with total emotion. I think it has been my best discourse till now. I remember intense happiness, each word said, every gesture made, and even the jokes of encouragement to us to enter the font of icy water. I was baptized with two of my four children, one being too young, and the oldest refusing until two weeks later when he overcame the personal problems of a thirteen-year-old boy.

But in the midst of our great happiness brought about by this choice experience, my mother was taken ill and was rendered bedridden by an illness which finally carried her away. Though it required much of my time to help care for her, I felt by no means like discontinuing, even temporarily, my discussions with the elders, from whom I was learning more of the gospel and with whom I shared the happiness of the truth and the hope of the resurrection. These were extremely sad and trying days, and I had to budget my time with precision, but thanks to the marvelous doctrine that I was learning each day and the consolation the missionaries gave me through their faith and their testimonies, I was able to face everything with courage.

The last day came, and my mother died; she simply stopped breathing. The family asked me to say a prayer, which I did, thanking our Father in heaven for the mother he had given us, and for the good things we had learned from her and the happiness we had received from her beauty and presence during all these years.

It is difficult to enumerate all that changed for the better in our family after we entered the Church. I see my sons growing with secure orientation, happy and steadily progressing each day. The oldest is already a teacher and a Sunday School superintendent, presiding in the meeting with authority. We have family nights regularly, and the result is always happy for each of us. The children sometimes bear their testimonies in church, and it touches my heart to hear their innocent purposes. As for myself, my life which before was empty is now full of the purest love and the most marvelous hopes. I see miracles all around me. And each time I pray, I feel more at ease and closer to my Father in heaven. I know that my prayers are always answered.

One day I reached a point where I felt that the period of my stay and my activities in Cruz Alta were coming to an end. I turned to the Lord in prayer, and I asked him to send me wherever I could serve him best. While I was praying, I received the inspiration that I should request my re-engagement in the diplomatic service. I submitted the petition without too much hope, as it is really a most difficult thing to obtain, but a position better than that for which I had applied was offered to me!

I realize that besides serving my country, this was a call for me to serve the Church. This was an answer from the Lord to my fervent prayer, in which I had asked him to give me an opportunity to do as much as I could possibly do, so as to deserve the blessings he is giving me every day as well as those blessings he has promised me.

As soon as I arrived in Colombia where I had been assigned to organize and direct the Brazilian Cultural Center, I was asked to teach the investigator class in Sunday School and to serve also as president of the Relief Society. When the branch president set me apart to fill these responsibilities, he said to me: "Sister, the progress and development of your private life is closely related with the progress and development of the Church of Jesus Christ, not only in Colombia, but all over the world." I do not know what the meaning of this prophecy is, but I do know that I am ready to serve the Lord as I am asked to do.

I know God lives, and I know Jesus Christ lives and stands at the right hand of God. The angels' aim is the only guidance I want for my children. There is no other life I wish to live, nor any other love that would so fully satisfy my soul; and there is no other hope. It is true, it is all true!

My soul lives on its knees, and I can find no words to express my gratitude for the wise and merciful action of the Lord when he sent to me on that sad and boring Sunday afternoon two of his missionaries to teach me the gospel. God bless them!

JOHN S. STALEY

A CATHOLIC MONK FINDS GOSPEL BROTHERHOOD

The brotherhood of a monastic order was John Staley's life for twenty-five years, the expression of his deep commitment to the Catholic faith. But the outward serenity of monastic life was in sharp contrast to his growing feelings of doubt and discontent about many features of that life. Finally, with permission, he left the order and sought to make reforms with the greater freedom of a layman.

The account which follows portrays the excitement of the quest as John Staley seeks—and eventually finds—his long-dreamed-of Christian brotherhood. Reading it, the Church member finds himself a little more appreciative than before for the great gospel truths he tends to take too much for granted.

As a professor of Sociology at Brigham Young University, today John Staley brings to his students a combination of sound professional training, deep religious and intellectual experience, and firm conviction respecting the restoration of the gospel through Joseph Smith.

To recount and share this expansive experience of being baptized, receiving the gift of the Holy Ghost, and being sealed in a temple of God for eternity by the sacred ordinance of marriage is an ever-growing source of joy. I hope that my testimony of our Father's goodness will renew your experience of finding the gospel, or anticipate the joy that will be yours in embracing membership in The Church of Jesus Christ of Latter-day Saints. Thus I share with you my impressions of the gifts of peace and joy that I especially wish to bear personal witness to as a grateful member of the Restored Church of Christ.

My Life as Catholic Priest and Monk

Two little boys, orphaned at ages five and seven, were reared by the Benedictine monks of the St. Vincent Archabbey in Latrobe, Pennsylvania. One grew up to become the father of a large Catholic family of 13 children, of whom I was second youngest. The other boy grew up to become Abbot, or head, of that religious community.

The Abbot was my boyhood hero and was a frequent visitor in our home, as was the bishop of the local diocese. Good Catholic parents often encourage a son or daughter, who has the inclination, to dedicate his life to the Lord's service. Such a desire sprouted in my heart. As a lad of twelve I left the family circle to join my uncle at St. Vincent's, where there was a prep school, liberal arts college, and seminary for the training of Catholic priests.

After two years of college, I took my first triennial vows as a Benedictine monk. There were five of these vows:

1. A vow of poverty—that all the money I would ever earn would go directly to the St. Vincent monastery for the education of youth.

2. A vow of chastity—that I would never marry nor partake of physical love, in the belief that this state was a higher level of sanctity than marriage.

3. A vow of obedience—to obey the monastic superior or Abbot, because his will represented God's will.

4. A vow of stability—to be a member of the St. Vincent community of 240 monks and priests for the remainder of my life.

5. A vow of conversion of morals—to promise to attempt to rid myself of imperfections and seek for virtue, trying to become perfect even as our Father in heaven is perfect.

As a young idealist of nineteen I gladly renewed these vows each year, culminating with final vows as a monk three years later.

According to St. Benedict, founder of the order in the early sixth century, a monk is one who seeks God. I must confess that my knowledge was indistinct as to who and what God really was. This has been a lifelong quest.

In 1941, when I was twenty-five, my ordination as a Roman Catholic priest was witnessed by my community, family, and friends. Mother, in a surge of love for me and maternal pride in giving a son to God, had the diamond from her engagement ring set into the silver chalice I would use in the celebration of mass. It was a day of rejoicing.

As monks and priests we rose daily at 3:40 a.m. to pray, recite psalms, assist at mass, meditate, and study. At 8:00 a.m. we began teaching classes. The day ended with vespers and compline, the official night prayer. On weekends and holidays and during summers we assisted in parishes by saying masses, hearing confessions, and officiating at baptisms, weddings, and funerals, as well as other pastoral duties. I spent thirty-two years in this way of life, which I viewed as service to God and man.

About five years after ordination I began to experience some discontent and found that in my religious life there were things difficult to accept. However, in keeping with the vows, I did all that was required of me. Each year as we celebrated the Feast of St. Benedict I would recall what I had said to God on that day of final vows: "Lord, let me not be confounded in my expectations." But I became increasingly confounded and sometimes complained to God as Moses did when those expectations did not materialize.

During these years I was a member of the Liturgical Conference, an organization interested in modernizing the Catholic worship service, and of the American Vernacular Society which, after twenty-five years, was to be successful in obtaining Vatican approval for the use of English in the mass rather than traditional Latin.

By 1966 I was openly protesting in my monastic community against various practices in the system. I was made to feel evil for trying to bring changes for good. This weighed heavily upon me, and I formally applied for laicization, being convinced that the Catholic Church was in dire need of reform to render it relevant to the needs of mid-twentieth-century man. The church structure prevented me as a priest from taking any more action as regards reforms than I already had; so it appeared that I could be more effective in bringing about reforms as a layman. (The process of becoming officially a layman, with the approval of the Vatican, usually requires several years, during which time the priest is still bound by his vows.)

It was at this juncture that the Abbot agreed to let me continue my quest by founding a new community whereby I could, with some measure of freedom, experiment with my ideas for monasticism. I obtained a post-doctoral fellowship in sociology at the University of Pittsburgh. In February of 1967 I left St. Vincent with both gladness and sadness in my heart, sensing that never again would I be a resident, teacher, or priest there. I left St. Vincent at the age of fifty. As an expression of my desire for a declericalized priesthood, I was wearing a tie instead of a Roman collar and a suit instead of a monk's habit. My only possessions were a few clothes and books and an ancient car given to me by a friend. I felt much like a kicking infant emerging from the womb as I drove through the monastery gates.

The Search of a Troubled Priest

My fellowship at the University did not begin until September. For the interim period I had been invited to teach part-time at a remarkable place in Philadelphia, the Institutes for the Achievement of Human Potential, where new and successful ways of treating all types of brain-injured children had been discovered. I was enticed there by a friend's intriguing description of it as a place where "the lame are made to walk, the blind to see, the deaf to hear, and the boss lives in a stable." There I found the distinguished director of the Institutes living in the remodeled carriage-house of a sizable turn-of-the-century estate. The other buildings, including a huge old mansion, were used for research, diagnosis, and treatment of children—including those without brain-injury but who had reading problems—and for accelerating the learning of pre-school children. I met the staff of the Institutes, who were Christlike in their love for and devotion to children.

As a sociologist I was there to learn as well as teach—to learn how the concepts of the Institutes could be applied theologically and sociologically for the achievement of human potential. On the second day I met Mariellen, a mature graduate student. We met while observing the evaluation of a severely brain-injured child.

I conversed with Mariellen over the ideals that had led her to the Institutes, about her own brain-injured mentally-retarded son (now a young man of 22), and about the experiences she had had in working with such children. She was interested in my reasons for coming to the Institutes. As we talked later, I shared with her some of my enthusiasm for the Catholic Church. I had observed a spirituality that shone from her and the great desire she had to help problem children. As a priest, I thought she would make a splendid nun to found a new order for this work. My objective was to persuade her in this direction.

For "bait" I gave her a copy of *The Divine Milieu*, written by Pierre Teilhard de Chardin, an eminent French Jesuit priest and physical anthropologist. That book describes the author's concept of how man is gradually moving toward divinization. I considered it to be the most precious statement from a twentieth-century Catholic and thought that it surely would interest Mariellen in Catholicism. I anticipated the excitement this book would generate in her.

A few days later she returned the book to me and smilingly said, "I enjoyed the book—parts of it sound as though they might have been written by a Latter-day Saint." Never having heard that term before, I had to ask her, "What is a Latter-day Saint?" She replied, "I'm one, a member of The Church of Jesus Christ of Latter-day Saints. Sometimes we are nicknamed Mormons."

From that point our discussions in theology veered sharply away from Catholicism as she adroitly led me into a new search by quoting from Lorenzo Snow, a past president of her Church: "As man is, God once was; as God is, man may become." My spring was unsprung! President Snow had outdistanced Teilhard by a spiritual light-year! His was the most profound set of words I had heard in my life—and all my adult years had been spent studying theology, philosophy, and sociology!

While Darwin spoke of the evolution of the body of man; while Spencer spoke about the development of the family and social institutions of man; while Teilhard spoke about the spiritual evolution of man; here Lorenzo Snow—to me, an obscure Mormon leader of the 1890's—had taken the teachings of Joseph Smith (which antedated Darwin's *Origin of the Species*) and said that not only is *man* progressing toward deification, but that *God himself* has gone through this process. What a vision this opened! What excitement shook me! This struck at the heart of my difficulties as a Catholic theologian and sociologist. Snow's statement went further than anything I had dreamed. I had considered Teilhard as one of the great contemporary thinkers, and here in twelve short words was a vision that eclipsed his farthest reach.

As a seminary teacher at St. Vincent, I had been searching for a way in which doctrine might develop to meet the emerging needs of men rather than stand still. It was in this search that I had discovered the writings of Father Teilhard, who had captured the minds of many intellectuals in France as well as America with his scientific and theological perspectives. The Catholic Church would not permit his avant-garde writings to be published, and in fact they were not published until after his death in the 1950's. He had written about this idea of the continuous development in another book, *The Phenomenon of Man*. Also, I had read deeply another Catholic theologian, John Newman, in his *Development of Doctrine*. I had come to appreciate the search for the opening up of doctrine that would respond to the knowledge and development of man.

The central theme of the restored gospel stated aphoristically by President Lorenzo Snow went far beyond Teilhard and Newman. What I found here, I found in every one of the aspirations that was troubling me: the search for a new kind of priesthood, the search for a new kind of worship, the search for a new kind of perspective on man. Here, in the teachings of The Church of Jesus Christ of Latter-day Saints, was a vision of man on an ascending, expanding, open-ended spiral of eternal progression. This is *dynamic*, developmental, as opposed to the *static* closed circle of organization accepted by prevalent Christian thought.

This explained the inherent but frustrating desire in man to be what he is not yet; the boy to be Superman; the teenager to become a hero; the Greeks and Romans to aspire to godhood; the deification of mortals in Oriental religions. This desire for divinization is inborn in man, then, but it took modern prophets of the Lord to affirm this as revealed truth.

During this time I was commuting on alternate weeks between the Institutes in Philadelphia and the new monastic community being established in the ghetto northside of Pittsburgh. Other Catholics and I were forming an inner-city mission to the poorest of the poor while we were searching for answers of relevancy in our out-dated church. *Commonweal,* a layman's magazine which is spokesman for the disturbed Catholic, has published many articles and reports about the "troubled priests" who are seeking a better way to serve God, even though that way increasingly is causing them to forsake their priesthood. I was truly a troubled priest— happy for the vocation I had, but troubled in the pursuit of it. In that pursuit, I was looking for a way in which worship would come more spontaneously and directly out of the hearts of the faithful; that would allow each member to share his encounters with God and Christ.

Mariellen had electrified me by discussing the statement of President Snow. Now it was my turn to seek a similar reaction from her about a paper on "The Sacrament of Matrimony" that I had read in Denver back in 1946 at a meeting of the National Liturgical Week. The paper declared that the sacrament of marriage did not take place at the altar, but in the very intimate and sacred act of marriage itself. For this I was removed from my position as a seminary teacher for several years. In 1959 I was invited to give this paper again and this time it was received with a standing ovation from the seminary class that would be ordained the following year.

Mariellen agreed with my views, but I was disappointed in her reaction. She then proceeded to open for me a vista of the doctrine of celestial marriage taught by the Latter-day Saints as contained in Section 132 of the Doctrine and Covenants. This gave insight on one of the most pressing problems I had experienced as a sociologist and marriage counselor. As a former college chaplain, I knew too well the dissatisfactions that exist concerning the Catholic theology of sex and marriage. I thought I had come a long way in my own thinking until Mariellen explained the appealing doctrine of celestial marriage, in which a worthy and loving husband and wife can have their union sealed for time and eternity instead of "until death do you part."

Finding a New Community Instead of Founding One

Mariellen invited me to attend a Sunday School at the Philadelphia Ward, and I responded in the spirit of ecumenism. This was the first non-Catholic service I had ever attended. I went hoping to find ideas to use in my experimental community.

I found many things. Instead of a depersonalized mass of two thousand, I saw a group of perhaps two hundred people. I saw a boy of sixteen pronounce words of blessing on the symbolic bread and water for the sacrament, something I first did at the age of twenty-five. A youth of twelve distributed the sacrament. I noticed the reverent, humble manner in which the congregation received this. I heard a ten-year-old girl give a short talk from the pulpit, followed by a young woman. A college student played the piano for singing that was led by a white-haired matron. Two different men, in business suits, gave the opening and closing prayers spontaneously. Another conducted the meeting. I was awed by this involvement of the laity. So many had taken key parts instead of just one professionally trained man in ecclesiastical garb running the entire ceremony. This seemed to be worship on a higher level. It opened my eyes to a new reality.

After the opening assembly, the congregation dispersed to classes. Mariellen led me to the Gospel Doctrine class where the teacher, a young man, elicited lively participation from his adult students. This, after what I had just witnessed, so impressed me that I whispered to Mariellen, "Is this some kind of special service that you have once a year or so?" "Oh no," she quietly laughed, "it's done this way every Sunday." Although I was a stranger, I contributed to the class discussion and was listened to with interest.

After the service, many were reluctant to leave. I had been used to those two thousand worshippers walking solemnly into a big urban church, and forty-five minutes later filing out with scarcely a nod to anyone. Here I found people eager to share with one another. I find this in almost every Latter-day Saint service—what we sociologists call "primary relationships," a deep sharing of self with others. That first day in the Philadelphia Ward, I discovered many things that I was eager to take back to my monastic experiments in Pittsburgh. I did not realize it just yet, but I had found the kind of community I had been yearning and searching for, far beyond the dimensions of which I had dreamed.

In the worship service of The Church of Jesus Christ of Latter-day Saints I found a priesthood that is shared by all worthy men of the Church, beginning with age twelve, and wearing neither special vestments nor insignia. I discovered that, according to their various offices, they carry a gentle but strong authority to pray, teach, administer, heal, and to bring order among their families, wards, and stakes. I was witnessing the kingdom of God in action.

Later I was to read this in the Doctrine and Covenants, a book of modern revelation, in Section 121:

> . . . the rights of the priesthood are inseparably connected with the powers of heaven, and the powers of heaven cannot be controlled nor handled only upon the principles of righteousness.
>
> That they may be conferred upon us, it is true; but when we undertake to cover our sins, or to gratify our pride, our vain ambition, or to exercise control or dominion or compulsion upon the souls of the children of men, in any degree of unrighteousness, behold, the heavens withdraw themselves; the Spirit of the Lord is grieved; and when it is withdrawn, Amen to the priesthood or the authority of that man. . . .
>
> We have learned by sad experience that it is the nature and disposition of almost all men, as soon as they get a little authority, as they suppose, they will immediately begin to exercise unrighteous dominion.
>
> Hence many are called, but few are chosen.
>
> No power or influence can or ought to be maintained by virtue of the priesthood, only by persuasion, by long-suffering, by gentleness and meekness, and by love unfeigned. (D&C 121:36-37, 39-41.)

I saw this gentle priesthood, this priesthood that allowed man his free agency, exemplified that first day by the bishop of the Philadelphia Ward. It was wonderful to behold.

Before I left the chapel that day, one of the seventies (a priesthood calling specializing in missionary endeavors), put a blue Book of Mormon in my hand, admonishing me not to accept his word that it was true but to read it and pray over it in Christ's name, and promising that it would be made known to me whether it was truly the word of God. (This exhortation appears in Moroni 10:4-5.)

That afternoon Mariellen and I were discussing the Book of Mormon and she said, "Just as the New Testament is an enlargement on and supplement to the Old Testament, so the Book of Mormon is to the entire Holy Bible." This challenged me. I opened the book and began to read. It did read like scripture. It had a poignancy, a ring of truth; it reached into me as scripture should. It was direct and plain.

Later, as I finished reading the Book of Mormon, I saw it as a tying together of the Old and New Testaments; as a new witness that our Lord, Jesus Christ, is the Son of God. It helped me to understand the gospel as I never had before. It opened a great new body of revelations, the end of which is not yet. I never read this book but what I pray. I love to read and reread of such wonderful things as the faith of the brother of Jared, of such magnificent men as Lehi, Nephi, Alma, Benjamin, Ammon, and Mosiah—men who stand with like faith, love, and greatness as the best known biblical figures. This is another book in which to read the words of Christ as he taught the gospel, this time to the ancient peoples of the Western Hemisphere—the "other sheep" he referred to in the Book of John.

Mormon Elders Teach the Gospel to a Catholic Priest

Mariellen soon invited me to listen to two young elders give a series of six discussions about the gospel. My first reaction was that this was taking the ecumenical spirit too far, but I had a feeling that God was doing some wonderful things these days, and so I consented.

She introduced me to two college-age missionaries. They were sincere, direct, and had as clear a spirit as I have ever observed. There were no apologies, no invitation to argument. We prayed before each session. They invited me to pray, and I enjoyed these informal prayers. To my surprise, I discovered that these young men were adding to what I had known before. They said much that brought together the mosaic of pieces that had fit only loosely before, and they supplied a number of the missing ones.

I could accept the Mormon concept of God the Father, because in my studies of the Bible I had come close to this concept myself. But on the third session the elders talked about an apostasy, which meant that the early Christian churches had abandoned the purity of the gospel by taking away, adding to, and changing the teachings of Christ; and because of this, the authority of the priesthood was removed from the earth by God.

They told me that there had been a full restoration of the gospel, including authority of the priesthood, over a century ago when Joseph Smith was called by the Lord to be a prophet and to usher in the dispensation of the fulness of times. They cited all this with conviction and clarity, but I would listen to no more, and said: "I can believe that Joseph Smith was responsible for translating the Book of Mormon, but I can't believe that the good Catholic people I have known all my life did not have the fulness of the gospel." I could not accept their statement. The implication was that my Catholic baptism and priesthood were not valid. I could not abide this either, and bade them good-bye without making an appointment for any further discussions.

Unknown to me, that evening Mariellen and the elders, rather than argue the issue with historical facts, went to the Lord in prayer. I also felt prompted to pray about it. One of the underlying reasons for my dissatisfaction as a priest was that what I had been given in Catholicism was not enough. I had tried the system all my adult life, and must honestly say I found it failing in many areas.

Then I recalled a Jesuit priest at Notre Dame University, Father John McKenzie, who was head of the American Catholic

Theological Society. In his book, *Authority in the Church,* he had been saying approximately the same thing as the Mormon elders. McKenzie wrote that in the third century at the time of Constantine the authority in the Roman Catholic Church seemed to degenerate. The organization was somehow corrupted, left without its pristine purity. I, myself, had interpreted that corruption as being part of the pagan residue, though I now have a different view of it. I began to think more openly about McKenzie's study, a study that nearly caused him to be condemned as a heretic by the Archbishop of San Antonio.

Another disturbing factor came to my mind. Benedict of Nursea, founder of my monastic order, had left Rome in the sixth century in protest against the corruption there. He, too, was a reformer. I realized now that Rome had been Christianized for about two hundred years by the time Benedict withdrew. I began to question why he left, and it now struck me that the corruption he witnessed against was not in paganism but in the Catholic Church itself.

A study I had made as chairman of the monastic policy committee came also to mind. More than sixty-five per cent of my brother monks were troubled with psychosomatic disabilities such as ulcers, diverticulitis, migraine, or leaning on the crutch of alcohol. It came to me that the cause of these difficulties was a system of human relations that had been built on a defective vision of the gospel, a gospel tainted by apostasy.

My observations came into sharp focus. I know it was God speaking to me as a result of prayer. Arguments and facts from Mariellen and the elders alone could not have swayed me from my Catholic loyalty to believe that an apostasy had taken place.

The next day I told Mariellen quietly: "You know, I've been thinking about it, and I believe there really was an apostasy. When can we proceed with the fourth discussion?" However, let me make it clear that at no time had I any intention of leaving my church—the priesthood, yes, but not the Catholic Church itself. I loved my church. I was wed to it, and sought for reform within much as a husband seeks aid for a sick and ailing family.

Visit to an LDS Home Evening

On my first visit to the Philadelphia Ward I noticed that the babies cried differently. It puzzled me as a sociologist and a student of the family. The answer came as I later visited a family home evening of a young Latter-day Saint couple. I was delighted by the warmth and love and joy that radiated from the group. Everyone was involved. They sang. They had some spiritual lessons. They played games. They were close in love. Fear was outside. The strong loving part of the father reassured them. Here seemed to be the modern version of the strong Early Jewish family with its patriarchal priesthood welding the family members together. Social theorist Amitai Etzioni points out that coercive and instrumental authority (which uses people as things) alienates its subjects; persuasive authority binds in warm relationships (active society). The high premium placed on freedom and free agency struck me.

My Twenty-fifth Anniversary as a Catholic Priest

Instead of a considerable celebration of my twenty-fifth anniversary as a Catholic priest, I decided to just have a quiet luncheon with my family at a brother's cottage. My only present was a triple combination of Latter-day Saint scriptures. It was given to me by Mariellen, and was to play an important part in my coming to the commitment step.

My Decision to Marry

Before I had any intention of becoming a member of The Church of Jesus Christ of Latter-day Saints, I, along with other members of the Pittsburgh community, had declared that celibacy impeded both spiritual and human development. I went to my superior at Latrobe to seek his blessing on my intention to marry Mariellen. I had and have great confidence in him. He is truly a great man (he has since become head of the Benedictine Order in Rome). After I opened my heart to him, he responded by giving me a blessing. This he did as a person approving the decision of another person. I also visited my family and apprised them of my plans.

Baptism, the Gift of the Spirit, and Marriage

"A reed shaken in the wind" best describes me during the week before my marriage. (We had unwittingly set as our wedding date the 11th of July, the anniversary of my making solemn vows in the Benedictine order!) We prayed each evening together. The night before, I was in great apprehension. Was I going squarely into the jaws of Satan? We prayed. As we prayed, a warm, comforting spirit came over me. I found myself uttering words that did not seem to emanate from me. Words that gave me peace and joy as I said them: "I want to be baptized; I wish to be baptized."

Early the next morning I called the bishop of the Philadelphia Ward and asked if I might be baptized and receive the gift of the Holy Ghost *as well* as be married. There was a long pause, and then his reassurance. How grateful I was for his discerning spirit!

On the way to be baptized at the Philadelphia Ward, I went through another agonizing anxiety: "Am I being deceived by the devil? Am I on a greased slide into hell?" As these fears tormented me, I opened the triple combination Mariellen had given me. This book of eight hundred pages opened to Section 131 in the Doctrine and Covenants. Had our Father in heaven sent an angel to reassure me I would probably have questioned his origin. The probability of this book opening to that page was far too low for it to have been an accident. I read:

> In the celestial glory there are three heavens or degrees; and in order to obtain the highest, a man must enter into this order of the priesthood [meaning the new and everlasting covenant of marriage]; and if he does not, he cannot obtain it. (D&C 131:1-3.)

Needless to say, I did not receive many wedding gifts, but this priceless one of assurance from our Heavenly Father that exorcized my fear will always be highly treasured.

To receive the holy ordinances of baptism and the gift of the Holy Ghost and to have Mariellen as my bride were almost too much for this vessel of clay to hold. It was the great day of my life up to that time. It was only eclipsed in joy by the later occasion of our being sealed for time and eternity in a temple of God.

My Patriarchal Blessing

To have one's spiritual DNA Chart read to him by one inspired of God, by a patriarch of the Church, as I did, is an indescribable experience. To have one's ancestral ties open up, to have the sure knowledge of belonging to the tribe of Ephraim and Joseph—what a joy, especially after having given a series of nine talks on Joseph of Egypt to a Carmelite Community one year before! To be assured of health and many vocations to special work in our Father's vineyard was and is a source of the mixed feelings that mark the typical Latter-day Saint: a profound gratitude for all that God has done for me and a deep concern that I have not done enough to further his kingdom and climb that great ascending spiral that keeps opening up to new, exciting vistas.

Encounters with Death

As a Catholic I had gained a sense that the hour of death was a moment of truth, that if I ever left the Catholic Church I would tremble at the hour of death and wish for a Catholic priest to come and administer to me. With heart surgery not many years behind, I twice found myself in the crisis of facing death. On both occasions I was administered to by elders of the Church. On the first occasion I was in Albert Einstein Medical Center with a critical coronary insufficiency. In his concern, the Abbot from my former community flew over to Philadelphia to visit me. On his arrival I indicated my gratitude for his desire to help me, but I was visibly at peace and calm and I voiced what was within me. In his openness he later received me at the monastery where I had opportunity to speak to him of the restored gospel. I thought I detected in him a wistful envy of what I had discovered.

Spiritual Progress

With the clear direction of the Word of Wisdom I found myself making great physical and spiritual progress. My colleagues from the monastery were perhaps most surprised and impressed by my ability to refrain from alcohol and coffee. But the growth in prayer, the new-found interest in scriptures, the rich opportunities to be involved in the callings within the ward, the ordination to the Aaronic and Melchizedek Priesthoods, finally holding the office of elder—these spelled out my real growth.

The experience of the fast and testimony meeting seldom leaves me dry-eyed. To hear brother after brother, sister after sister, reveal God's personal working in their lives is one of the richest spiritual experiences open to man. It was what I sought in monastic community. It is what I found in the community of The Church of Jesus Christ of Latter-day Saints.

It seemed to me I used to have many dreams of what I wished I could be like in following Christ; the principal difference now seems to be that I can do these things through the power of the Spirit. True, it requires a continual covenanting and renewing of covenants with our Father, but the ability to do so is much more readily available.

My Marriage in the House of the Lord

Progress is programmed by love. The highest level of development is dependent upon being sealed for time and eternity in temple marriage. As it was promised in my patriarchal blessing, Mariellen and I went up to the temple the year after my baptism to take out our endowments and have our marriage sealed.

Instead of body and soul being anti-bodies as envisioned by Augustine, the restored gospel explains that all spirit is matter, only more refined. (Again Doctrine and Covenants, Section 131!) Physical love, therefore, is not ignoble (or at least venially sinful). Rather, it is the advanced spirit (God) leading the less advanced (his children) to higher realization.

For years as sociologist and theologian I had probed the meaning of marriage, of sex and love. In the great revelation of the restored gospel given in the endowments, the mystery of man and woman, of love and marriage, of the divine plan of progression to divinization opened to me with breathtaking clarity. The successive covenants with God ending in the eternal covenant of marriage both moistened the eye with joy and sobered the spirit with the awesomeness of the responsibilities involved.

All my life I had been in pilgrimage to the House of the Lord, and now I finally could say: "Lord, you have *not* confounded me in my expectations. You programmed me for joy, and you have not withheld those things necessary to possess it." What new meaning the pilgrim psalms took on for me!

Some Attractions in the Gospel

1. The universal need to continually develop, even to the point of becoming a God, climbing the path of the ascending, expanding, open-ended spiral originally traced out by our Father.

2. The priesthood of Christ with its great power but gentle persuasive authority and the divine presence it effects in the affairs of men.

3. The centrality of love marking human relations from the family to the ward, from the neighborhood to the international community, where brother is brother in the preexistence and the earthly existence—it not only makes babies cry differently, but makes adults encounter differently.

4. The great vision of love and marriage and its wedding to development and joy; the freeing of the celibate for celestialization.

5. The simplicity, warmth, and divinizing power of the worship that strips away the dross and human appendages and allows communion with our Father and our brothers and sisters in ever-developing measure.

6. The clear vision of the meaning and path through these latter days, so dim before, and now so clearly lighted through the opening up of the meaning of Isaiah and Ezekiel, John the Revelator, and the Mormon prophets and scriptures, especially the Doctrine and Covenants.

My Testimony

I know within me that Jesus Christ stands at the head of this, his Church, and by its medium gives the members the plan and power to become sons of God through eternal progression.

To me Joseph Smith was the most vigorous of the great prophets, who as a young farm boy encountered the whole of Christianity, Protestant and Catholic, and redressed it with the clear and plain truth of the restored gospel as he opened up this dispensation of the fulness of times.

Within me I know that each succeeding president of the Church is indeed a living prophet of our Father in heaven and offers us continuing guidance, revelation, and direction in these days of great perplexity for man.

I witness to these things with joy of spirit in the name of Jesus Christ.

EDNA K. BUSH

BLESSED WITH THE COMFORTER

"What a tall tale—an angel with gold plates!" That was Edna Bush's response to the Book of Mormon story she heard on Temple Square in 1939.

But eleven years later she met the book itself, as lady missionaries introduced it to her in her New Orleans home. She began reading it from curiosity—but when she reached verse three on page one she had received "a verification from within."

The book was to become the great study of her life. Her insights into it and her deep conviction of its truth inspire others. In missionary and study groups she is a popular teacher, lecturer and writer.

At first unable to be baptized, she suffered the loss of the Spirit which had brought her great peace and joy. Spiritual strugglings and earnest prayers were her recourse. She rejoices that today she is blessed with the Comforter.

The people that walked in darkness have seen a great light; they that dwell in the land of the shadow of death, upon them hath the light shined. (Isaiah 9:2.)

They also that erred in spirit shall come to understanding, and they that murmured shall learn doctrine. (Isaiah 29:24.)

Yearly, thousands of visitors to Salt Lake City walk away from Temple Square unimpressed with the Mormon story. I was such a visitor in 1939. What a tall tale—an angel with gold plates!

Having grown up in the south where I'd heard spirituals sung about golden slippers for walking the golden streets, I immediately thought, "Oh, sure the plates were gold! The slippers were gold, the streets were gold. If they'd said the words were written with diamonds, it would have been an even better story!" So with the "superior" intelligence I possessed at the time, I walked away—to hear no more about the Mormons for years.

What happened to me in the interval included some government and civic work in Washington, several moves, the production of two sons, the development of a real rattlesnake disposition, and the obvious loss of the "superior" intelligence I'd possessed in Salt Lake City.

I began to look about for something. In Atlanta, my home town, I visited a book fair held in the city auditorium. The building was packed with what seemed an endless number of publisher's works, but I came away disappointed at not finding the something my spirit was seeking. What I was seeking I didn't know, and soon forgot.

Another move, and my family found ourselves in New Orleans. Our two chaise lounges in the living room typified what life was like for me in 1950—a lazy, leisurely life, juleps flavored with garden mint, and so on. Mornings were for working in the strawberry and flower beds, for filling crawfish holes with camphor balls; afternoons, when the heat was greater, were for straightening the house. Shorts and halter were the usual attire. Our pretty, grey brick home, with its verbena-lined sidewalks, its gardenias, azaleas, camellias, shrimp plants, and poinsettias, made New Orleans a dreamy place for me.

I still had the rattlesnake disposition, though, and should not have been shocked but was to hear our poetical pre-schooler, Larry, reciting:

> Little Bo Peep has lost her sheep
> And can't tell where to find them.
> *"Leave that alone!!!"*
> And they'll come home
> Wagging their tails behind them.

Another shock came when Les, Junior, our second-grader, innocently asked, "Mother, what people do you stand?"

The question made absolutely no sense to me. "What do you mean?" I queried.

"Well," he responded, "You can't stand Mrs. Jones, and you can't stand Mrs. Smith, what people *do* you stand?"

What was I teaching my children!

We were attending no church. I tried several but quit them all. One church could have passed as a country club; another, humble and sweet, offered no challenge. I thought, "A God who could create a world as complex as ours would certainly have more to *his* church than Sunday meetings and Friday-night suppers."

One church I attended required healings for membership. I could have passed that test, but the requirement seemed wrong— at odds with God's love for all men. Why not require one to speak in tongues, or to see visions, for membership? There were, of course, no longer such things as visions; though I did feel that we moderns were treated unfairly since we face greater dangers today than people of ancient times when God was occasionally around. You can see, a "Luciferite" had intercepted most of the Mormon guide's message I should have heard on Temple Square—nothing came through about a recent visit from God; just that queer story about an angel with gold plates.

"Why aren't you taking the children to Sunday School?" my husband asked one day.

"I will when I find the right one," I replied, without a thought that I'd ever find one.

"Do you think you have to set up your own?" he asked. I almost supposed I'd have to.

So Sundays were spent swimming or crabbing at Lake Pontchartrain, picnicking at Grand Isle, or sometimes just doing chores around the house. The days drifted by. The wonderful weather of New Orleans provided another reason for thinking the place a dreamy one.

Then there came a real dream—real and unforgettable. The dream contained a powerful message which had such an effect upon me that I wrote to the newspaper. My remarks appeared in the letters column. The message of my dream was that I had to contribute something in this life in order to attain a certain desired position in the life to come. This deeply bothered me. What contribution could a housewife make! The letter, having been published, now gives me the date of the occurrence–October 23, 1950.

Three mornings later, instead of my usual a.m. condition— scantily clad for gardening, rooms yet to be straightened—I was dressed in a pretty print pongee, and the house was tidy. There came a knock at the door. It took me a few minutes to reach the front. I arrived to find two young ladies walking away.

"Did you knock?" I called. That's when I met the Mormons again!

Obviously the girls had come quite a distance, walking. I invited them in to rest on the chaises. Instead they perched on the edges and began telling me their story.

Even though I had thought the Mormons gullible to swallow such an outlandish tale as they put out, still I had thought Salt Lake City beautiful and carried fond memories of my visit. After some conversation the girls asked if I'd like to buy a copy of their book. "They are pleasant, but just sellers of books," I thought. I experienced a deep depression, but I did not want the pleasant girls to feel as badly as I, so I made the purchase. They left, and instantly I was into the book.

The visit of the angel Moroni to Joseph Smith and Joseph's description of the angel's bodily appearance, as given in the pages on the origin of the Book of Mormon, made a striking impression on me. It was the first description I'd ever read that made an angel seem believable. Previously, angels and fairies had somehow belonged to a sort of never-never land.

I began reading strictly for curiosity. That I should ever be interested in the *Mormons* would have seemed farfetched indeed. What a surprise it was, then, to receive a verification from within when I'd reached only the third verse on page one. It seemed undeniable that Nephi was speaking the truth, that it was he who had made the record I was reading.

How many of Lucifer's spirits were assigned to me while I read, I may some day know. They were certainly doing nothing to let light through as I read the visions of Lehi and Nephi and the Isaiah parts. When I reached the statement attributed to Joseph of Egypt about a man named Joseph bringing forth a book, one spirit whispered, "And if you had written the book, *your* name would have been right there."

Curiosity kept me trying to find out who Mormon and Moroni (I called him *Moroney*) were, so I plunged on through the darkness. Finally I came to the Words of Mormon, where I met the two, but the account was too sketchy to be satisfying. I continued the search.

The Book of Mosiah—what confusion! I was completely lost, but I was intrigued with the dry bones and ancient ruins. With each page I turned I thought I'd learn their origin. (For the new reader, a hint: turn to the Book of Ether, in the back of the book. If I'd glanced at the footnotes I'd have solved the puzzle before I gave up on it, but how many first readers give heed to that voluminous collection?)

A charmer was the Book of Alma—the first half, that is. So forcefully did one of its messages come through that I later spent much time trying to find it again. If it interests you to learn what passage it was, it was Alma 32.

But the second half of Alma! Almost congealing were its bloody, endless wars. I didn't like that part at all, though today I find much meat in the accounts, for actions do make better sermons than words.

The "whodunit" story in the Book of Helaman was most interesting. But Samuel's sermon about the birth and death of Jesus—the effect of his birth and death upon nature—was such a divergence from anything I'd ever been exposed to that it was not difficult to believe the whispering spirit who was repeating in my ear; "This is wrong! Jesus in ancient America! It's sacrilegious!"

I read on. Third Nephi recorded the possible origin of Indian tribes. Here was something not at all hard to believe. Then chapters eight through ten, with the story of the terrible destruction in America, explained how the great Rocky Mountains could have been broken into the huge fragments I'd seen out west. That had nagged at my mind for years. So had another question: "Why doesn't man live as long as a dumb turtle when it is man who has the brains?" Third Nephi gave me the answer to that puzzler also—man is on earth for a test; it is unnecessary that he live a great length of time.

When I'd finished the accounts of Jesus' several visits to the ancient Americans, I could not have believed the story more if I had been one of the Nephites at Bountiful in A.D. 34. I felt a wonderful warmth as I read Jesus' words to those people. To have learned of Jesus' importance insofar as this planet and its inhabitants are concerned (Jesus, the Creator and the Judge) came as a terrific surprise, for I'd been taught only that he was a great teacher who lived and died long ago.

Fourth Nephi and Mormon's own small book brought sadness, again, and I concluded that wars would never cease until the return of Jesus. But I finally met Mormon and Moroni!

The Jaredite story, in Ether, answered yet another question for me, with its account of the premortal visit of Jesus to the brother of Jared. The theory that I'd come into existence at my birth to mortal parents had never been acceptable to me. The early part of Ether was a sweet, consoling story, but then came another account of complete destruction, plus warnings to us who live today.

Then came Moroni's own book, with its instructions, two letters from Father Mormon, and a marvelous sermon Mormon had given before his death. From these writings I learned much. The sermon indicated that not everyone was in unsatisfactory standing in Mormon's day, a fact easily overlooked when reading Mormon's small book. The letter in Moroni chapter 8 answered another matter I'd thought upon from time to time, the inappropriateness of baptizing babies. Obviously this mistake was being made even in Moroni's day, or Mormon would not have written the letter.

Finally, in the tenth chapter of Moroni, was a verification promised to the sincere reader. Without my even asking, a wonderful, burning testimony came to me. I put a thermometer into my mouth, thinking it would register 104 degrees (it registered normally), for there was a real, physical burning going on. I could feel the fire on my cheek with my hand. Without any question whatever, I *knew* the book was of God, not of man. How unspeakably marvelous! God had not forgotten man. And he promised even more knowledge to the believer.

Though I came away from my first reading of the Book of Mormon with a positive knowledge as to the greatness of Jesus Christ, I came away also with a knowledge of the greatness of my ignorance, and I was determined to go through the book again with a pencil to figure out those dark passages. But one pencil didn't do it. I switched to colors, marking what I considered to be important passages. Oh, the folly of that idea! The book is a riot of color; there were no unimportant passages. The result? Pure confusion. Today that copy makes an excellent visual aid as I try to explain to others the vast contents of the Book of Mormon.

Though I had no idea what the Mormons believed, I wanted to be where that book was. Those pleasant girls were visiting me regularly and my head swam from all the information they so easily brought forth. I had a deep desire to go right through the Bible. I remember excusing myself from the nomination of PTA president, with "Ask me next year; this year I have to read the Bible." What a storehouse of knowledge I'd been ignoring, and how stupid I felt that I didn't know whether Moses was Abraham's ancestor or vice versa, to say nothing of my ignorance as to where to find Chronicles or Corinthians!

I soon knew I had to be baptized. How strange! I'd always thought water baptism was for the great unwashed, not for the sophisticated souls. For the first time in my life, I *really wanted* to join a church. The gift of the Holy Ghost was something I deeply desired. I learned that the Church makes an unusual requirement for membership; in some cases written approval is required. This written consent or approval was unavailable in my case.

Soon the lady missionaries were transferred away; then a stream of elders came visiting. How many sets I sidetracked with my constant questions I don't know, but finally one said, "Let's have the lesson first; then we'll answer questions." Until then I never knew they'd been trying to teach me lessons!

Surprisingly one day — a sad, sad day — that wonderful warmth, the manifestation of the Spirit, was suddenly gone. What a period of bleakness and sorrow followed! How many tears I shed! I tried reasoning with God, "If it were up to me, I'd be baptized!" But there was no return of the Spirit.

After many yearnings and tearful prayers, a voice spoke to me in the night. "Study the beatitudes," it said. How odd, I thought. Those blessings are for people who have died and who were "those things" in this life. I used a thesaurus, and began making a list of synonyms for the words in the beatitudes. I was surprised to learn that "blessed" meant "happy," and "meek" (instead of meaning a milquetoast, which I would never be) meant "humble." I went on through the list. The Spirit whispered, "If you let these be your attitude, you will be happy." Beatitudes became: *Be* Attitudes! I typed the list, taped it inside a kitchen cupboard where it could be checked constantly, and tried hard to adjust my behavior. It was not long afterwards that the written approval needed for baptism was obtained.

While waiting for baptism, I'd been made president of the new Primary in New Orleans and had made many friends who rejoiced with me at the great news. For years I'd downgraded baptism, now I felt like sending out engraved announcements. But the strangest things happened on the big day when my baptism was to take place. Doors slammed, things fell, it was queer! There was no chapel in New Orleans at the time; we drove to Baton Rouge for the service. By now it was August, 1951. It was sundown when we made the trip. The beautiful pink of the sunset seemed a love message from heaven, and I was serenely happy. A couple of days later, I was confirmed a member of The Church of Jesus Christ of Latter-day Saints and *received again the marvelous warmth of the Spirit*, this time as a permanent gift.

Today I vividly remember my sorrow at the departure of the Spirit after the Book of Mormon verification visit. I remember the tears, but I treasure the experience for I know *doubly* what it is to be without the Comforter and to be blessed with the Comforter. How appropriate that name, the Comforter. It truly comforts— just as in my childhood, at bedtime, when I'd be knotted up with cold, and mother would add a comforter to the covers. What lovely warmth, how the tensions eased!

Like many another convert, I was certain my family and friends would be as overjoyed as I was to learn that Jesus had said much more than is found in the Bible, to learn that he'd been back to the earth in these latter days more than once. Enthusiastically I began telling them about my discovery and dispensing copies of the Book of Mormon. To my great surprise, they were almost totally uninterested.

At first I couldn't believe it. Sadness weighed me down. For quite a while I was like Peter in wanting to cut off ears, or like James and John who wanted to call down fire from heaven. Then I discovered that my nonmember friends were not alone in their reluctance to read the Book of Mormon, that many Church members had not read it. I wanted to shake such members and say, "Don't you realize what you have!"

Slowly I learned that this is not the way God operates. He allows man to make his own decisions, and forces no man to heaven. If man doesn't care to learn more about his Heavenly Father it is his privilege to have this attitude, though he will come under judgment for this lack of attention. It has been extremely difficult for me to understand this. I have mourned much in the process. Today, after nearly twenty years, I can almost accept the fact that what is, is. I pray often that my heart will not hurt so much about the lack of interest on the part of my loved ones. As for Church members, occasionally I have to stifle the urge to nudge them and cry, with Isaiah, "Awake! Awake!"

For years I searched Church publications for the writings of some other convert who'd felt the loneliness of being in a part-member family, but I found none. Perhaps someone who today is sorrowing over a similar situation may read these words and take courage to continue the struggle. From an Old Testament story I found a stimulant to help overcome the sadness. In speaking to

Samuel concerning the downfall of Saul, the Lord asked, "How long wilt thou mourn?" Then I realized there should come an end to mourning.

I have found comfort in working closely with God's word in the Book of Mormon, hoping someday to fulfill the requirement that I must make a contribution in this life. Realizing how little treasured is the Book of Mormon, I could see an opportunity to use my business training to make it more understandable through marking, simply, some of its passages. Finally, after years of searching and after coloring dozens and dozens of copies of the Book of Mormon, I have evolved a simple dissection study system, a system which has been found useful by not a few members, nonmembers, and missionaries. Perhaps that is my contribution.

If my large collection of marked copies of the Book of Mormon served no other purpose, it certainly furnished my two sons with an intellectual testimony of the truth of the book. Indeed a *seeker* after truth, an earnest *seeker,* would be hard pressed to ignore the seemingly endless detail which my almost twenty years of research has made so visual. With such research, errors would long ago have been detected, but each avenue of approach has strengthened my faith that Joseph Smith did not concoct the story but translated an ancient record as he claimed.

Alma 32, the chapter that shone through during my first reading of the Book of Mormon, declares that the word of God will expand the mind, enlighten the understanding, and enlarge the soul. It declares also that the word is delicious. I bear testimony to that truth. The book provides a marvelous route to personal growth and a magnificent means for gathering Israel, as promised by Bible prophets.

The Comforter, received upon baptism into The Church of Jesus Christ of Latter-day Saints, is a consoler and inspirer, and an ever present help in times of troubles and distress.

Though once I walked in darkness, today I see a great light. Though I erred and murmured, today I am continually gaining new understanding and learning much doctrine.

IMMO LUSCHIN VON EBENGREUTH

THANK GOD FOR THE MISSIONARIES

The spark which ignites the spirit of conversion differs with individuals. As much as anything, that spark for Immo Luschin von Ebengreuth was eternal marriage.

A full-time translator for the Church in Frankfurt, Germany, Immo is a well-educated man who speaks five languages and has studied both medicine and law at the University of Graz, Austria, his home town. He has always been deeply religious. Blessed with a happy marriage which they had deliberately oriented toward religion, Immo and his wife could not accept that that marriage must end at death. In their thoughtful and prayerful approach they found other basic problems too which were not answered by their Roman Catholic faith. For all that, they were reluctant to seek answers outside of their religion.

The following account tells how the missionaries' faith and persistence prevailed in providing the answers. "Someone had to be courageous and persistent enough . . . ," says Brother Immo Luschin, as his Church friends call him. "Thank God for the missionaries."

For several months prior to our wedding, my fiancee and I spent our evenings discussing every phase of our future. Among other things, we decided that we would make religion a very substantial part of our marriage. Our children, we felt, would have to be protected from the evils of the world, and this could best be done by making religion the foundation of our moral lives.

Both Helmi and I were Catholic, after the tradition of our parents and forefathers, which means, in our case, that we were

baptized when less than one month old. We attended Catholic
classes in school (because we had to), and went to church (only
when we were made to do so). Otherwise, we had no religious
activity, no reading of the Holy Bible, and after we were gradu-
ated from school, no going to church either. But because of our
commitment to each other, our religious activity increased after
marriage.

On the day of our wedding, a beautiful September morning
in 1947, we went to confession, partook of the sacrament of the
Eucharist, and were married, first at the registrar's, according to
the Austrian law, and then in the Catholic Cathedral, that is, the
Herz-Jesu-Kirche at Graz, Austria, our home town. From then on
we attended mass on Sundays, went to confession at least once a
year, and fasted on the day preceding Christmas Day and on Good
Friday. We tried to be in harmony with all the ritual injunctions
of the Roman Catholic Church. As our four children came along,
each was baptized within the week of its birth; later we taught
them to pray to our Father in heaven and went to church with them
every Sunday.

Previously, during the Second World War, I had been
required to serve in the German Army. My wartime experiences
were such that I could not but believe in a Divine Providence,
having been spared many times and under very unusual conditions.
All during these years, something within assured me that I would
not die before I would become the father of a family, and I always
felt that the Lord had given me that promise because of some
important task which might be mine in the future.

Compared with what we saw around us, ours was a singularly
happy union. Before we were married, Helmi and I had agreed
that there would be no divorce in our life. Moreover, we seemed
to be a little different from our friends in that we were probing
and questioning as to what the purpose of life should be. Many of
our friends seemed to have the attitude that life was given in
order that we get out of it what we could—namely, "eat, drink, and
be merry, for tomorrow we die." Enjoyment rather than joy, self-
assertion rather than righteousness, seemed to be typifying the
general attitude we encountered among our associates. Problems,

they believed, should be covered rather than solved, especially if the solving implied self-restraint. The most desirable thing was not to eliminate transgression, but not to *get caught* at it.

After some six years of continued happiness in our married life, I said to Helmi one evening, "You know, I don't believe that we shall be separated in the hereafter, as the priest who married us said we would be. We shall be together forever."

"But how could this be possible?" she asked.

"I do not know. But one thing I know for sure. If they don't have this kind of provision yet, they must invent it for our sake."

More and more we felt the need to protect our four children from the all-too-liberal influences of the world. Who, or what guidance, was going to help us select the right way of life for them, as well as for ourselves? This problem was constantly on our minds. Can our religion assist us in solving it? I started to read the Bible, because I hoped to find an answer there. Occasionally, I read from the Bible to my family.

Helmi and I discussed several aspects of our religion wherein we either disagreed with the officially accepted doctrine, or were not fully satisfied. There were also some passages of scripture which aroused my concern. I felt that there was inconsistency in what was written there, or at least that I was not intelligent enough to see past the letter and reach the spirit of the doing.

Then 1960 came. In March I had reached a state of mind wherein I felt distracted and worried about almost every aspect of life, and I decided to take a step which heretofore had not occurred to me. One morning, I entered a small chapel not far from my downtown office, at an hour when I knew no one would be there. I knelt and asked the Lord for his help. I came away with a feeling of peace in my heart—but still nothing happened, so far as I could see.

Life went on as usual. We were guests at two society weddings, and later found out that in each case the wedding date had been a little late. Our thoughts were heavy, because we wanted desperately to help our children avoid this type of experience. Yet, the society in which they were developing was condoning immorality more and more.

Helmi and I began to enjoy a very close association with Reginald, a former school friend of mine, and his wife. They were the parents of three children. This friendship turned out to be not at all what we had hoped it would be, namely, the pooling of information and experiences for the purpose of mutually improving our lives. Several times our social evenings with them ended the same way as did the evenings spent with our other friends: after meaningless discussions of meaningless topics everybody was spiritually enlightened only by some high percentage spirit out of a bottle.

On July 13, Reginald died suddenly. In the small hours of morning, after having spent much time in a bar, he had run his small car head-on into a big truck. Helmi took his children into our home for several days, caring for them while waiting for things at their home to get back to normal. During this same week, two young men called on her and wanted to bring her some religious message. They were clad in dark business suits and obviously were foreigners. Helmi did not listen to them, but agreed that they could return the next week.

The following week, the two young men returned. Helmi was watering and weeding the flower beds, and they persuaded her to be seated with them at a nearby table in our garden. They asked her permission to open the discussion with prayer. They asked her about her family, introduced religious matters, and started questioning her. Helmi warded off all inquiry by telling them that they should come back on Saturday when her husband would be home. They then again offered prayer. Helmi says, "This is the thing which impressed me most, and for many years will be stamped into my mind. They included me and my children in their prayer, asking him to bless us and to look after our needs."

I scarcely paid attention when, on Saturday morning, she told me that two young men, possibly Americans, would come at 2 p.m. and try to see me. At two o'clock I was in my downstairs workshop, working on a birthday present for Helmi, when the doorbell rang.

"Good day. We are missionaries of The Church of Jesus Christ of Latter-day Saints, and we have a very important message to impart to you," said one. He introduced himself as Elder Bryner and his companion as Elder Johnson.

"We want to tell you that there is a living prophet of the Lord today," he continued, "and that the full gospel of Jesus Christ has been restored in our day and age by a modern prophet, Joseph Smith." His German was quite good, although his sentences sounded as though they were rehearsed and somewhat worn out by too frequent repetition. His companion remained silent except when, after some inaudible exclamation mark in his friend's statements, he would utter, "Ik uais auch dahs dahs uahr iist," (meaning, "I, too, know that this is true"), spoken with a heavy American accent. As a linguist, I was particularly aware of these external matters.

I was not interested. I did not invite them in, even though it was raining cats and dogs outside. Not even their clear, bright eyes could move me to let them come in; neither did their purposeful sincerity, which I sensed. I was a Catholic, and I intended to remain one. Suddenly a thought crossed my mind. It must be a very humiliating task to go and preach religion, having every other door slammed in their faces, as I was about to do to them. I knew that my neighbors down the street were not going to listen to them either. Very embarrassing and most humiliating, I thought. Their payment could not amount to much, the way they were dressed. And yet they did their work. What power motivated them?

"Could you come and see me on Monday, two days from today, at nine o'clock in my downtown office?" They assured me they would. They also tried to give me some literature, which I would not accept.

Later that day, when the rain had stopped, I found in our driveway a small brochure, completely soaked. Its title was "Joseph Smith Tells His Own Story." Now it came back to me: These were Mormons, the ones connected with polygamy!

On Monday their exactness in meeting our 9 a.m. appointment impressed me favorably. I led them into my private office and invited them to sit down. One of them then said a prayer, asking the Lord to let His Spirit be with us. Elder Bryner then proceeded to embark on an apparently memorized recitation of a religious nature, using several sheets with stick figures on them to illustrate his argumentation. I waved these aside, cut short his presentation, and said to them, "Now, gentlemen, I don't want to offend you. I have read about your precious Joseph Smith and his own story. But before we go on, I should like to ask you a few questions."

"During our marriage, my wife and I have both felt that we should also be together in heaven, even though we fail to see at the moment how this is possible. What stand do you, or rather, does your church take?"

Elder Bryner reached for a book in a black leather cover, rapidly turned the pages, then read a few sentences to the effect that a marriage covenant, if entered into under the right conditions, could be sealed up for eternity. He explained to me a very convincing doctrine of his church on that matter.

I posed the next question: "If a child were born, and, without even a chance of being baptized, died, why should it be condemned to go to the kind of hell my church has devised for it? I simply cannot bring myself to believe that my Father in heaven can be as cruel and unjust as all that. What is the transgression of Adam to me? I do not believe in any original sin. I never had a chance to disapprove of anything our first progenitor might have perpetrated. By the way, do you really think God tempted Adam knowingly to bring about his fall? This would have been rather a 'Pontius Pilate' sort of behavior, wouldn't it?"

I was told that little children were redeemed from the beginning through Jesus Christ; also that Adam, in making his decision, was fully exercising his own free agency. Our discussion lasted three hours, until noon. I invited them to come again two days later, and then again, and again. There were more questions that had been vexing me.

"Do the rich and the poor, in your church, have the same opportunity to reach their salvation?" I asked.

I had a very special reason for asking this question. From what I had seen all around me, I had certainly come to the conclusion that a person who had sufficient means was far more likely to escape eternal damnation, or at least purgatory, than the other fellow with no worldly purchasing power to his credit.

"In my wife's and my opinion, it is a great sin to confess a transgression, to take penitence for it, knowing at the same time that one is very likely to commit it again and again. Should not true repentance consist of: being sorry, the restitution, the promise never to do it again, and then the asking of God's forgiveness?"

This question had been prompted by an experience I had had. About two months previously there had been a mass meeting at Graz, at which a famous Jesuit Father preached. Thinking he might be able to help me, I asked him for an interview. He agreed to meet me the next day. My problem was that, under the rule of the Catholic Church, a certain action on my part was considered a sin which I was obliged to confess, and I felt grave concern about it, but each time I confessed it to a priest I knew that I would do it again. How could I hope to extricate myself from this dilemma? This Father told me that he could not help me either, except that he was willing to grant me general absolution if I were to confess to him, which I did. But after that, I felt more doubts and qualms than ever before. Something must be wrong in this reasoning, I thought.

I had another question to put to the missionaries. "In the Bible I have read about Cain and his offering not having been respected by the Lord. From what I can find in Genesis, I cannot but conclude that God must have been partial or arbitrary in his dealings with these first sons of Adam and Eve. Could you explain to me the full story or meaning of this?" They could. Out of a book in a black leather cover.

The elders knew an answer to every question I had; and what is more, it was the right answer, the one I had been looking for all along. I felt as if I was approaching my old home town after many years of absence. At the conclusion of their second visit the elders asked me to kneel with them and offer the prayer, which I did.

They gave me a Book of Mormon, the army edition. I had asked them to let me have it in English. I read the Book of Mormon in the course of one night. At that time, I told Helmi of my recent experiences. She was somewhat surprised. I guess I showed much enthusiasm explaining to her what I had learned. The missionaries gave me a German edition of Lowell Bennion's book, *An Introduction to the Gospel*. Helmi asked me to read it to her, and after each chapter we discussed it. It gave us many of the answers which we had been looking for practically all our lives.

I do not know just at what time I was converted. It would be hard to tell. But when she asked me, "Now, do you really believe all this story about an angel and golden plates and so on," I sat there for some time and tried to decide whether I did or not. Is it any harder to believe in a prophet who wears a necktie and a modern hat than a prophet with a long white beard who lived many centuries ago? I told Helmi I really believed it to be true. Perhaps I did not so much believe it as I *hoped* it was true, and this was my reasoning. All the answers I had received from the elders were what I knew they should be. So for the rest of the doctrine and teachings of this church, I just hoped they would be true also. Everything was so consistent, so appealing to every fiber of my being.

On the 14th of August the elders asked me to quit smoking. I had been using tobacco constantly for twenty-five years. Several times I had made an attempt to give it up, without success. They told me I could do it with the help of the Lord. On that day I smoked the last cigarette of my life.

We were used to a church tax in our homeland. They told us (and it was Helmi who in her practical way put the question to them) that nowhere was there a government tax levied to help support their church. Instead, they said, members of their church were privileged in that they had an opportunity to return to the Lord one-tenth of their income annually, or in other words, to pay their tithing. And it was Helmi who from the day of our conversion supported and strengthened me in making myself and my family eligible to receive all the blessings that come through keeping this commandment.

August 28, 1960. This day I was baptized by Elder David F. Johnson, and was confirmed a member of The Church of Jesus Christ of Latter-day Saints by Elder Lowell L. Bryner.

Helmi was baptized two weeks later; the two older children, Astrid, 12, and Hanno, 10, after three months of instruction, were baptized in December of the same year. Gero, who was then 7 years old, and Iris, 5, were later baptized by myself when they were old enough to be baptized.

The most important day in my life, and in Helmi's life, was the 21st of August, 1961, when we were sealed for time and all eternity in the temple which is located in Switzerland. And I know that if we prove true and faithful, we will not be separated in the hereafter.

I knew this was the truth; I had known it all along. But someone had to come and show it to me by breaking down the walls which tradition and other worldly considerations had built around me. Someone had to be courageous and persistent enough to disregard my reluctance to do as the Lord wanted me to do.

Someone had to tell me. Thank God for the missionaries.

IRVING H. COHEN

A JEW FINDS THE TRUE MESSIAH

Born an orthodox Jew, Irving Cohen was converted to the gospel with the help of a fellow officer while serving with the armed forces in Korea. This involved his making a radical change in the attitudes and understandings that were a part of his traditional background. Both as stake missionary and high councilor he has continued to bear a fervent testimony on all possible occasions and this has resulted in many other conversions to the gospel.

A dentist by profession, Irving Cohen lives in Schenectady, New York. He here gives the moving story of how he found the true Jewish Messiah in the person of Jesus Christ, and of some of the trials and joys this discovery brought him.

I was born into an orthodox Jewish family in Brooklyn, New York. My parents had five children. I was their third child and first son. Like so many of the Jewish boys at the time, I attended Hebrew school and was prepared for my bar-mitzvah—the ceremony held for a Jewish boy when he reaches the age of thirteen and is considered a man by the Jewish community and he can then stand before the congregation and say certain prayers.

Right after my bar-mitzvah, as I continued to have my Hebrew lessons, I asked my rabbi: "Why is it that the Jewish people haven't had a prophet for two thousand five hundred years? I don't expect a hundred prophets, maybe not even ten prophets. But I do expect one prophet. Surely there must be one Jew somewhere who is worthy to be a 'nauvey' (prophet)!"

My rabbi could only shrug his shoulders at the question. I then took the problem to my wonderful father and he, too, could not answer the question. All the evidence for the fact that there would be no more prophets referred to the words of a Psalm (22:1): "Eli, Eli." "Eli, Eli" has the ring and cry of how the Jewish people have fallen away from God's graces and how they have been persecuted, burned, and spat upon throughout the ages, and how they yearn to be back again as God's chosen people.

I entered college a few years after my bar-mitzvah, and one of my classes was a course in philosophy. All term long we argued, "Is there or isn't there a God?" At the end of the term, each person in the class was required to write a thesis. My thesis was that God once lived but had died. I reasoned in this way: Supposing a great architect constructs a building. The building stands five hundred years, but the man who created it, the architect, dies at the age of one hundred. Somebody else comes along two hundred years later and discovers the building. In studying it he realizes that it took an intelligence to create the building. Similarly, I realized that it took an intelligence to create the world. But since the Jewish people haven't had a prophet for two thousand five hundred years and the Christian people basically can't claim a prophet for almost two thousand years, and since the world is in a horrible condition, the God who created this world must have gone off and died. I was sure that if he still had control over it, he wouldn't let it be in its present state.

So much for my philosophy! But as the years went by I tried, at least, to do the right thing by my fellowmen.

In the course of time I became a dentist. In 1953 I received a call to serve my country and I complied gladly. I was made acting company commander for one hundred dentists at Fort Sam Houston. My platoon leader, a dentist from Phoenix, Arizona, named Junius Gibbons, was somehow different from anybody else around him. Here were ninety-nine other dentists, and this one young dentist stood out head and shoulders above the rest. Not that he was taller; but his character shone forth. I said to myself, "This guy is different, and I want to get to know him so I can see what makes him tick." Later on he told me that he had

had similar thoughts about me and had watched for the opportunity to approach me.

One day we were waiting to be interviewed by the commanding general, and Dr. Gibbons said to me, "Captain, what religion do you profess?"

I said, "I don't profess any religion; however, I am not ashamed to say that I am of Jewish background. But I don't believe in Judaism. I have searched Christianity and I don't believe in Christianity either—not the Christianity that I've found. I have also studied the other religions of the world, and I have come to the conclusion that religion is a man-made situation. If I'm going to be religious, it is not going to be in a man-made religion. I want to find God and worship in his religion, if there be such a thing."

He took me by the hand and said, "I'm a fellow Israelite."

I said, "You mean you're a Jew?"

He said, "No, no. If you are a Jew, you are probably of the tribe of Judah, and I'm of the tribe of Joseph. These are two tribes within the House of Israel." He continued to pump my hand.

He stunned me by that remark. I went home, and I said, "You know, I met a fellow who claims he is of the house of Israel, and he is not Jewish. How do you account for that?"

"Oh, don't pay any attention to him," was the reply. "Everybody is trying to get into the act!"

But I asked myself right then and there: "Does Gibbons know something that I don't know?"

Junius Gibbons and I were among those assigned to the Far East theater of operations, the Korean conflict, and we met next at Ft. Lewis, Washington. I saw him at breakfast. We were confined to the base, because we were leaving within twenty-four hours.

I said to him, "I'd like to hear more about what you have to say about the Israelites, the Jews, and the tribe of Joseph."

He was very anxious to help me. He said, "Fine. After breakfast let's find a little quiet place where we'll have some privacy, and we'll go over some of the Bible."

After we found our spot, Dr. Gibbons told me, among other things, that he had another book, similar to the Bible, called the Book of Mormon, and that he believed that book to be scripture also. And he told me a little about the origin of the book.

I said, "You mean to tell me that you had a prophet by the name of Joseph Smith, and he had the courage, the temerity, and the audacity to write these things in a book?"

"Joseph Smith didn't write them, he only translated them," he replied. "But here's the book."

I said, "You know, I'd like to have a copy of that book."

"I'll give it to you on one condition . . . ."

"Okay," I said, and I reached for my wallet.

"No, no. That's not the condition," my friend Gibbons said, handing me the book. "Just promise me you'll read it."

I made the promise. By this time it must have been about one o'clock in the morning. My plane took off about 3 a.m., so I said goodbye to Dr. Gibbons and, taking his book, I went off for Japan on the way to Korea.

When I arrived in Korea, I didn't feel that I wanted to do what the other officers were doing—gambling, drinking, carousing. I had this book, the Book of Mormon. Reading it was worthwhile to me, but I was not about to believe that it came from the source it claimed. I thought I could disprove it by finding obvious errors, so I spent my time reading.

As I read the Book of Mormon from cover to cover, there were parts that I didn't absorb too much. I decided I'd better compare it with the Bible, so I asked one of my chaplain friends for a Bible, which he gave to me.

Now I read through the Old and New Testaments for the first time in my adult life. I was looking for errors, for contradictions between the Bible and the Book of Mormon. I couldn't find any the first time through, so I knew I'd just have to try harder. I read the Book of Mormon for the second time, and this time I began to understand a little more about what was going on. Then I decided I had better read the Bible through again, and this I did, from cover to cover, for the second time. And then I went back to the Book of Mormon for a third time, and within the last chapter I read this:

> Behold, I would exhort you that when ye shall read these things, if it be wisdom in God that you should read them, that ye would remember how merciful the Lord has been unto the children of men, from the creation of Adam even down unto the time that you shall receive these things, and ponder it in your hearts.
>
> And when ye shall receive these things, I would exhort you that ye would ask God, the Eternal Father, in the name of Christ, if these things are not true; and if ye shall ask with a sincere heart, with real intent, having faith in Christ, he will manifest the truth of it unto you, by the power of the Holy Ghost.
>
> And by the power of the Holy Ghost ye may know the truth of all things.
>
> (Moroni 10:3-5)

Obviously that is written for a Christian. Here I am, Jewish. So I would like to reword verses 4 and 5 for my Jewish readers.

"And when ye shall receive these things, I would exhort you that you would ask God, the God of Abraham, Isaac, and Jacob, in the name of the Messiah, if these things are not true; and if ye shall ask with a sincere heart, with real intent, having faith in the Messiah, he will manifest the truth of it unto you, by the power of the Ruach Elohim (literally translated, 'the Spirit of God,' and in Christian terminology, 'the Holy Ghost'). And by the power of the Ruach Elohim (or the Spirit of God, or the Holy Ghost) you may know the truth of all things."

This hit me, and I said, "If this is a book of God, then Irving Cohen is entitled to a revelation." But I had two problems.

Problem No. 1: The book said I had to ask in the name of Jesus Christ, and I didn't know whether or not Jesus Christ *was* the Messiah.

Problem No. 2: I could say a prayer for bread, a prayer for food, but there was no prayer in Hebrew covering the Book of Mormon. I was stuck!

At this time I was the regimental dental surgeon. My regiment had been moved down to the Isle of Koji where we were guarding the prisoners picked up on the 38th parallel. For some reason a great many operations were coming up and I didn't have enough supplies. I went to my colonel, and I said, "I need supplies desperately. I have a friend over in Pusan (on the southernmost tip of Korea), and if you will give me a three-day pass, I will get my supplies." He granted me permission for a three-day leave.

At Pusan, I went to see my friend, Junius Gibbons. He gave me my supplies and asked me, "By the way, did you keep your promise?"

"Yes, I did," I replied proudly. "I read it three times, not once." And then I told him about my two problems.

He said, "All right, Irving, I'll tell you what we'll do. Let's go through the Old Testament, the book of your people, and cover all of the prophecies concerning the coming of the Messiah, and then see where we go from there."

The Old Testament is a record of my ancestors, and the Jews still believe in the coming of the Messiah, so I agreed. We began with Deuteronomy chapter 8, verses 15 and 18; then we read from the Prophets, and finally we came to the 53rd chapter of Isaiah. I am going to change some of the words here again; I'm not going to take any of them out, but I am going to add a few words for clarity. Since the Old Testament is the book of the Jews, wherever it says "we" or "us," it means the Jews; wherever it reads "he" or "him," it refers to the Messiah.

> "Who hath believed our report? and to whom is the arm of the Lord revealed? For he [the Messiah] shall grow up before him as a tender plant, and as a root out of a dry ground: he [the Messiah] hath no form nor comeliness; and when we [the Jews] shall see him, there is no beauty that we [the Jews] should desire him.
>
> "He [the Messiah] is despised and rejected of men; a man of sorrows, and acquainted with grief; and we [the Jews] hid as it were our faces from him; he [the Messiah] was despised, and we [the Jews] esteemed him not.
>
> "Surely he [the Messiah] hath borne our griefs, and carried our sorrows: yet we [the Jews] did esteem him stricken, smitten of God, and afflicted.
>
> "But he [the Messiah] was wounded for our transgressions, he was bruised for our iniquities: the chastisement of our peace was upon him; and with his stripes we [the Jews] are healed.

"All we [the Jews] like sheep have gone astray; we [the Jews] have turned every one to his own way; and the Lord hath laid on him [the Messiah] the iniquity of us all.

"He [the Messiah] was oppressed, and he was afflicted, yet he opened not his mouth: he [the Messiah] is brought as a lamb to the slaughter, and as a sheep before her shearers is dumb, so he [the Messiah] openeth not his mouth.

"He [the Messiah] was taken from prison and from judgment: and who shall declare his generation? for he [the Messiah] was cut off out of the land of the living: for the transgression of my people [the Jews] was he stricken."

(Isaiah 53:1-8)

As we arrived at about this point in the Old Testament it seemed to me that a brilliant light started to come into the room where we were. I am not able to explain *how* it happened; all I know is that it did happen. And with this light came the Ruach Elohim, or the Spirit of God. Something leaped inside of me, causing me to jump up, and I shouted to my friend, Junius, "I've got it! I've got it!"

He asked, "What have you got?"

"I know now that *Jesus* is the *Messiah*!"

I found myself sobbing with joy and relief, and, for a few minutes we were silent. My mind raced. "Why do the Jews not believe in Jesus as the Messiah?" I asked myself. Because they are taught this idea by their parents. Were their parents there at the time? No. How did *they* know what was right and what was wrong? They failed to believe because they were also taught not to believe. Were their grandparents there? No. But because somebody made a mistake two thousand years ago, do I have to close my eyes and make the same mistake? In college I had always been taught to recognize truth. My parents had always taught me to be truthful and to defend truth. If God reveals to me that Jesus is the Messiah, am I supposed to close my eyes and go along the wrong path just to be agreeable with my mistaken ancestors? NO!

In New Testament times the original followers of Christ were all Jews. They could be compared to the radical element, while those who did not believe in Jesus as the Messiah remained the conservatives. As the years went by, those who accepted Christ became known by the new name, "Christians." The conservatives kept the old identification, Jews. But both of these groups had originally been Jews. And if one of my "Conservative" ancestors two thousand years ago could not believe that Jesus was the Messiah, then do all of his descendants have to follow that same tradition? Suppose Jesus is the Messiah. The question is, are we, the Jews of this generation, going to be big enough to accept him?

The Jewish people have an expression which they use in the synagogue: "Vawohovtah adonoi eloechchaw, becall levovchaw, vebecall nafshechaw, becall moadechaw," which in English means: "Love the Lord with all thy heart, with all thy might, with all thy mind, and with all thy soul."

Now that I knew that Jesus was the Messiah, I *did* love him with all my heart and soul, and with this love, the Ruach Elohim bore testimony to me (and still does) that indeed the Messiah is Jesus Christ. But I still didn't know how to pray. So Junius said to me, "If you want to pray, you begin by getting down on your knees."

"Just a minute. I'm a Jew, and Jews never get on their knees, not even on the Day of Atonement."

"But," he said, "if it's good enough for a prophet, it's good enough for Irving Cohen. Right? The Old Testament tells us that Daniel 'kneeled upon his knees . . . and prayed, and gave thanks before his God . . . ,' even after King Darius had decreed that anyone who did so would be cast into a den of lions." (Daniel 6:10.)

And I agreed that if it were good enough for a prophet, it should be good enough for Irving Cohen. So Irving Cohen got down on his knees.

Then Junius said, "And when you pray, address the one to whom you are praying; after all, God is your Father."

The Jewish people pray "Auvenu Malkaynu," a chant meaning "Our Father, our King." "God *is* our Father," I thought, "and what righteous father doesn't want to hear his child talk to him directly?"

Junius said, "You address your Father in heaven." And then he taught me something—something I had never known before. He said, "You have to thank God for what you already have, because unless you appreciate what you already have, why should God give you anything more? See, he'd be spoiling you." (A wise parent doesn't want to spoil his child.)

It was at that time that I started to appreciate my blessings, which I had never done so fully before; I had not been properly aware of them. Junius said, "If you appreciate your blessings, you are in a position to ask for more, as long as it is done in righteousness. So then you ask whether or not this Book of Mormon is true; and then do it in the name of Jesus, the Messiah, Amen."

I said good night to my buddy, went into my own room, and then for the first time in my life—alone, by myself—I went down on my knees, and I made a prayer something like this: "Oh God, the God of Abraham, Isaac, and Jacob, forgive me for not knowing better in my youth. I am only interested in doing the right thing now. I don't want a man-made religion. I want a God-made religion. So I'll make you a proposition: If you will show me that this Book of Mormon is true and that the Mormon religion is your religion upon the earth, I'll take every opportunity to teach this to others. On the other hand, if this Book of Mormon is a false book, and you reveal this to me, I'll expose these Mormons as a bunch of frauds up and down the earth. And I say this in the name of Jesus, my Messiah. Amen."

I don't just *believe* the Book of Mormon is true; I *know* it. It was shown to me that night that God lives; that Jesus is the Messiah; that there are entities called angels; that there are prophets upon the earth restored to the house of Israel—not just to the Jews, but to the rest of the tribes of Israel as well.

The Book of Mormon, from the tribe of Joseph, is another record equal to the Bible, which is from the tribe of Judah. Now I understood what Ezekiel meant when he wrote:

> The word of the Lord came unto me again, saying, Moreover, thou son of man, take thee one stick, and write upon it, For Judah, and for the children of Israel his companions: then take another stick

and write upon it, For Joseph, the stick of Ephraim, and for all the house of Israel his companions; And join them one to another into one stick; and they shall become one in thine hand.

(Ezekiel 37:15-17)

In Ezekiel's days they didn't have books. Instead they took a piece of parchment, wrote on it, and wrapped it around a stick, and this they called a "stick." The stick of Judah which Ezekiel mentions is the Bible, written principally by Jews, descendants of Judah the son of Jacob. The stick of Joseph is the Book of Mormon, written by descendants of Judah's brother, Joseph, in America.

As soon as I knew the Book of Mormon to be truly a book of God, I immediately knew that there were troubled days ahead. Nevertheless, I had to keep my promise. That meant joining The Church of Jesus Christ of Latter-day Saints and devoting my life to telling others about the gospel.

Upon being released from the service, I finally returned to my home in Brooklyn, New York, where my Jewish wife gave me an ultimatum: "Either give up your Christian Mormon nonsense, or give me a divorce."

I didn't want my wife to divorce me, and I didn't want to lose my infant daughter. I also did not want to go contrary to God's will. I realized that I was in a real dilemma. What was I to do?

Then the thought came that I should follow the same pattern that I had learned. "Ask and it shall be given." I went to my knees and asked Heavenly Father what to do. I needed guidance. As I was thus in prayer, it seemed that a distinct voice began to speak to me, and with it came the power of the Ruach Elohim or Holy Ghost.

I immediately picked up a pencil and began to write that which I heard. It is recorded as follows:

"My son, when I created this earth and put the human family upon it, I did so upon the principle of free agency. Therefore, if your wife insists upon exercising her right to do so, don't attempt to prevent her. However, let the record show that *she* obtained the divorce.

"Further, whatever you give up in my behalf I will return it upon your head, seven-fold. Since you will lose your little girl, the future will return seven for one.

"I, the Lord God, further promise you, that upon reaching the age of maturity, your daughter will leave her mother and come and join her father."

Well, the years passed, and during that time my Jewish wife did obtain the divorce, and I remarried. This new union has now produced the seven children which were promised—plus one more. And after sixteen and one-half years of separation, my daughter came to me in July, 1970.

I bear my testimony that the Book of Mormon is true, that God *lives*, and that he will answer the prayers of anyone, provided that that person wants to do his will—not seventy per cent of his will, not eighty per cent of his will, not even ninety per cent of his will, but one hundred per cent of his will. This is the prerequisite for us as it was for Moses. If you are willing to do his will one hundred per cent, you are entitled to receive an answer to your prayers, just as I did and still do. For this I am humbly grateful. This testimony I bear in the name of Jesus, your Messiah and my Messiah. Amen.

BILL WAIT

TRUTH FROM A BROTHER

*Not everyone receives the gospel through formally-called
missionaries. Sometimes it comes from a friend or a family member. Bill Wait received it through his older brother.*

*At first, however, he rejected it. "Tough, irreverent and
worldly," in the U. S. Navy in World War II he had no need for
religion and was embarrassed by his brother's conversion. Returning to civilian life he continued his search for "happiness" with
the same attitude.*

*Bill Wait held out against the truth for seven years. This
unembellished story of what made him change and how he found
true happiness in Jesus Christ is not only of great intrinsic interest
but will serve to encourage Church members whose loved ones
have so far not felt to join them in their allegiance to the gospel.*

When I was a kid, preparing for the weekly worship service
was a hectic ordeal in our home. As the meeting time approached,
shoes were still unshined, shirts were without buttons, ties were
wrinkled, and tempers flared. Our suits were made of burlap
interwoven with straw. The coarse fiber was irritating to tender
skin, so many of us wore our pajamas under our Sunday suits.
Arriving at church late, angry, and wrinkled, and smelling of
Shinola shoe polish, we would sit in our assigned front row seats
and brace ourselves for the fire and brimstone from the pulpit and
the crashing thumps from the elderly deacons sitting behind us.

My brother was more spiritually inclined than I. He studied his New Testament and endured the minor frustrations. As I grew older, I swore I would never attend church again.

One Sunday afternoon, after having made this vow, I sat with my friend, Jack, in his living room, reading the Sunday funnies and listening to Glen Miller playing "In the Mood." The music was interrupted as we received news that Pearl Harbor had been bombed by the Japanese. Our lives changed rapidly. Families and friends were separated, and the secure routine of life was abruptly changed.

My brother, two years older than I, quit high school and joined the Merchant Marine. A strange feeling of fear and nostalgia welled up in my heart as I stood in the early morning fog on the San Pedro water front, waving good-bye to my brother as he entered the gate to board his ship. Then for two hours I waited there in the fog for the Pacific Electric street car to take me home.

Weeks later, we received a phone call from New York. My brother was leaving his ship and coming home on a motorcycle. He arrived home suntanned, and filled with stories of great adventure on the high seas and across the plains of the western states. Within weeks he was gone again, this time with the United States Navy, as a seaman aboard destroyer escort on convoy duty in the North Atlantic.

Many ships were being sunk and many men were dying. My brother's greatest desire in life was to be married, and he was afraid that he might be killed in the war and never realize that dream. He had read in the Bible which he carried with him that there was no marrying or giving in marriage in heaven. He feared this meant that if he were killed he would never realize his greatest dream. As he stood on watch through the cold, dark, stormy nights, he would pray to know if this were true. After many long, lonely hours of deep and sincere prayer, he received a direct revelation that even if he were killed, he could be married in heaven.

This spiritual experience was so overpowering that he began to search for a church that taught this doctrine. As his ship would put in to port, he would buy books on different religions and study them through his tour of duty at sea. Soon he was transferred to a torpedoman's school in Rhode Island. After graduation he was transferred to Barbers Point on the Island of Oahu. One day he took a tour of the island.

The bus stopped at the Mormon Temple in Laie, and the tour group entered the bureau of information. As my brother stepped inside, his eyes fell upon a rack of pamphlets on the wall. One was entitled "Eternal Marriage." Taking a copy, he ran back to the bus and read it through tear-filled eyes. The Holy Ghost bore witness to him that he had found the truth that he had so diligently sought.

Upon returning to the naval base, he sought members of The Church of Jesus Christ of Latter-day Saints. He read the Book of Mormon, received a testimony of the gospel, and was baptized and confirmed a member of the Church. Overwhelmed with joy at his new-found truth, he wrote home and to me.

By this time, I was in New Guinea aboard a rusty old Navy ship. I, too, had quit high school and left home on my seventeenth birthday. I was homesick and discouraged, for I had left thinking that I would become a Navy hero aboard a destroyer or a submarine. But I was swinging around the hook in Madang, New Guinea, and cursing the heat, the ship, and the war. My brother's letter to me arrived with a package. I had hoped for goodies from Hawaii, but out dropped a book of scriptures. I was embarrassed in front of my friends to be receiving such a package, for we were tough, irreverent and worldly men. That night, I placed that Book of Mormon and some equipment of my shore-based days in the sea bag, and in the dark of the night I dropped it over the fan tail and gave the gospel light the "deep six." My search was for happiness, and I thought that it was not to be found in church.

My parents, knowing little of the Mormons, were shocked by my brother's decision and offered little encouragement to him. My feeling was that he had suffered too much of the pressure of war and had cracked under the strain. To me, church was an escape from life or an opportunity to make a living. I was embarrassed that a brother of mine had turned to religion.

The months rolled into years, and finally the war was over. My brother went home, and within a short while he was called on a full-time mission for the Church.

I had many months yet to serve on my enlistment, but finally we were all home as a family unit. I had been embarrassed in explaining to friends that my brother was a missionary. My concept was far different from what he had experienced. It was now my turn to hear, firsthand, his testimony and the plan of salvation. He wanted me to be baptized and join him in the kingdom of God. I was frustrated and disturbed by his strong desire. I tried to avoid him and continued my search for "happiness."

I had joined the Los Angeles Fire Department and was living the "Life of Riley." I had good pay, many hours off, good health, many friends, and could spend all of my time and money in the pursuit of pleasure. I was living at the engine house at the time, and I envied the firemen who went home to wives and families when relieved of duties. They, in turn, envied my freedom and lack of responsibility. But, inside, I was slowly dying because life was a meaningless rat-race.

The Korean War had begun. Friends were being called away to the horrors of war. As the empty days wore on, I became more and more discouraged. There was no apparent reason for my despair; I had everything that the world can offer—except happiness.

One night as we responded to an alarm of fire, a friend of mine, reporting from another engine house, fell off the tailboard of his truck and was killed. The alarm was false, and the futility of this tragedy, the return of war, and my futile search for happiness weighed heavily on me through the remainder of that night. When I was relieved of duty the next morning, I walked the streets of Los Angeles to where my friend had died.

Here, on Skid Row, as the smog hung heavily in the air, I found the tragedy of death which is a lack of reverence for life. All about me there was the stifling stench of sin. Obscenities were crudely written on the walls of the ugly buildings. Drunks were lying on the sidewalks, and the paddy wagon was making its morning rounds. The newspapers on the racks gave detailed accounts of the battle dead in Korea, and my thoughts filled me with despair.

I walked down the street and prayed to God to know why I was alive, and with all the energy of my soul I told him that I wanted a reason for life, or I wanted death. And, at twenty-four, I would have welcomed a release from mortal life.

But in answer to my sincere prayer I was overwhelmed with a desire to read the books that my brother had been urging me to read for the past seven years.

Now, each morning as I left work I went to the library and read the Book of Mormon, the Doctrine and Covenants, the Pearl of Great Price, and the New Testament. I knew that what I read was true; the Holy Ghost bombed me with the gospel of Jesus Christ, and I knew of a surety that the words were true. I was filled with despair at the exquisite memory of the wasted years of my life in search for happiness. But at the same time I was filled with an even greater joy, with the sure knowledge that God lives, and that Jesus is the Christ, and that Joseph Smith is a true prophet of God.

I began attending church, where I found not only the love of the Latter-day Saints, but also the love of the girl who was to become my eternal mate. Soon I was baptized and confirmed a member of the Church by my brother who had tried patiently and long to bring this great truth to me. Not long after, he baptized and confirmed my mother and my father. Soon we were sealed for time and all eternity to one another. A far greater security than I had ever known was ours. The true happiness which I had sought was found in its only source—a testimony of the gospel of Jesus Christ.

CLIFFORD J. BARBORKA, JR.

"HIRED" BY THE LORD

Material wealth, social position, worldly pleasures—these things have always been a threat to righteousness. Clifford Barborka almost succumbed to them.

His wife, the talented singer Melva Niles, accepted the gospel first. His resistance to it caused much conflict between them, and this tension was not eased by his health impairments caused by his heavy smoking and drinking. How was God going to reach down and lift a life like this?

The Lord's hand is indeed evident as the story unfolds. Today, many thousands of Church members and nonmembers alike from coast to coast have seen and enjoyed the programs presented by the talented Clifford and Melva as they serve their full-time informal mission. In this way as well as during their formal stake mission, they have borne to multitudes the fervent gospel testimony they feel.

For their talents and services, this couple formerly received an annual income in six figures. But as the reader clearly sees, their real success and happiness came when they were "hired" by the Lord.

When Melva Niles and I first met in 1947, she was starring in "Song of Norway" and had accompanied the show on its national tour. As we progressed towards marriage she made great strides in her career. By the time we were married, in 1949, her manager was Mr. Edwin Lester, director of the Los Angeles Civic Light Opera Association, and he had just "sold" her to Cole Porter for his new show, "Out of This World." Melva's income was up to $1500 per week. Fortunately, Melva has always been first a wife and second a career woman, especially after our two sons were born. This attitude is rare among talented women.

By 1956 Melva was recognized for her outstanding talent in both East Coast and West Coast theatrical circles. She had become a member of the Junior League and was a constant contributor to and participant in charitable causes. She donated her time to handicapped children and children's hospitals, made a benefit recording for Multiple Sclerosis, and so on. Personally, socially, and professionally, her life had been one of accomplishment and growth, and she was very much a part of the world and worldly ways.

In the meantime I became Midwest Sales Manager for John Blair & Company, which was the leader in its field and the first radio-television station representative firm to pass the $100 million gross figure. In 1958 I became vice president of that company, Director of Midwest Operations, and a member of the board of directors. Soon I would become the fifth largest stockholder of the company.

I mention these and other matters here, not for purposes of self-aggrandizement, but rather to set forth the background of our lives as they were when the gospel found us. Educated in midwestern private schools, and very much a part of the world both personally and professionally, I had never even heard of the name, "The Church of Jesus Christ of Latter-day Saints," and I knew of the Mormons only as a group headed by Brigham Young in a historical exodus to the west. My father's background was Catholic, my mother's family was Methodist, but we had long since fallen away from any formal religion.

For Melva and me, 1956 certainly was a great year, and it seemed to be the staging year for even greater growth. By 1957 we would enter our first of five years in which gross income would reach six figures. In short, the world was our oyster, for to us at that time it seemed that we had all that any couple could possibly desire.

One sunny day in July of 1956, my phone rang while I was in the midst of a most important meeting; Melva had called to tell me that she had been talking to two young men who told her about another young man who said he had seen God the Father and his Son Jesus Christ! This was so incredible to me that I told her to "get them out of our apartment and do so at once, and they are *not* to come back." This was the beginning of our personal Armageddon.

To Melva, this was the moment of truth for which her soul must have been thirsting, because she received an immediate testimony that these young missionaries were telling the truth. Subsequently she met regularly with them. Even I settled for two meetings at later dates. At one of these meetings, I tried to point out errors in the missionaries' teachings and presented an opposite viewpoint. Then I invited a personal friend, an Episcopalian priest, to have dinner with us and the young missionaries so that Melva might compare the learned with the unlearned, be brought back to the facts of life, and thus stop asking me to get involved. How well I remember that night! Intellectually, the priest dominated the young missionaries; however, I told Melva afterwards that I believed the two young men more than I did my long-time friend, the priest—but that, with all our other commitments and responsibilities, we could not get involved in a church.

Melva continued to go to church with the missionaries on most Sundays and occasionally to Relief Society. However, by worldly persuasion and reasoning I was able at this stage to argue her out of a firm commitment, to prevent the total involvement of baptism and membership. During this period I was asked by Isaac Smoot, the mission president, to speak to the missionaries on the subject of salesmanship, which was my specialty. I look back now and realize that while speaking to these young men I had an unusual feeling that could only mean one thing—a testimony.

My plan had been to demonstrate to the missionaries sample door approaches, showing them how they could get into more homes, how they could hold the attention of their prospects, and then how to present the material efficiently and effectively. As preparation for my presentation I read and re-read the *Joseph*

Smith Story which was the material the missionaries would be using. This pamphlet vaguely disturbed me. But it was not until I made the presentation before the assembled missionaries that I had the startling reaction to its message.

Suddenly, as I spoke, I felt as though I were alone, apart from the group which had become a blur in front of me—I felt levitated, disconnected from the floor. My fingers and toes tingled. I can recall this experience almost precisely, not because I analyzed it and understood it at the time; I was baffled! Once the sensation had passed, I concentrated on dismissing the whole thing as unusual but inconsequential. I turned my back on the first of three such testimonies.

I had graver things to think about! It was also at this time that my doctors gave me approximately ten years to live unless I changed my way of life. Life for me embraced a great deal of social activity including much professional entertaining. Every day I smoked three-and-a-half packs of cigarettes and drank from ten to fifteen drinks. Among my health impairments, I had developed a diseased liver, emphysema of the lungs, and high blood pressure—and I was only thirty-three years old. Life certainly had its conflicts.

After many pressures and arguments, I finally allowed Melva and our older son, Cliff III, to be baptized in 1960. At this point I began to lose my firm grip on Melva and the family, as our lines of communication began to pull apart. I discovered that in the highly-charged social atmosphere of New York, and more specifically Bronxville, New York—a very restricted suburban community covering about one square mile in area—our sons were beginning to experiment in undesirable behavior. It was also the year 1960 when I turned my back on another testimony.

It happened in a plush restaurant in New York City. A business acquaintance (who incidentally happened to be a good Mormon) was seated with me, and we were discussing uses of various sales tools.

"Do you *really* believe that Joseph Smith actually saw God?" I asked him without preliminary discussion on the subject. He then solemnly bore his testimony to me that he knew that Joseph Smith did indeed see God. I shook my head in disbelief and wonder that such a sensible man as my friend would embrace such fantasy! He patted my hand and told me that I would understand it all better after I had become a member of the Church! A highly charged sensation surged through me and again my hands and feet tingled. But I was unwilling to recognize or admit that these experiences were witnesses of the Holy Ghost.

My interests were in material gain and not in changing our way of life. Nevertheless, a strong sense of disenchantment was setting in on me as to the manner in which we were earning our living. The more I came in contact with the Church, the greater this disenchantment became, and combining this with the fact that Melva could not save our boys alone and that they were beginning to drift, I knew that something had to be done to improve the situation. Thus it was that in 1961 I sold my interests in John Blair & Company and became an individual entrepreneur. This allowed me more time with my sons, but nevertheless as a family our lives were terribly discordant. Melva and I drew further and further apart. I would send Melva, the boys, and our household help to church by limousine, and then have them picked up just before final song and prayer, as I wanted them home as quickly as possible. It seems so ridiculous now that I wasted so much precious time and built so many frustrations into our lives, with so much at stake spiritually.

Melva made a tragically prophetic statement shortly after she was baptized (I did not attend her baptism). She said that if I continued to stay away from the Church and did not take it seriously, we would lose everything. I did stay away and I did procrastinate with my inner feelings, and her prophecy was true in so many ways.

I remained opposed to joining my family in the Church. In fact, I would not admit believing any part of it. Nevertheless, I accepted, even volunteered, involvement in projects where my theatrical acumen would be useful. The members were grateful for the assignments I accepted in the production of Promised Valley, the Mormon Arts Festival at Columbia University, and the World's Fair Singing Mothers. I did not resent any of the time spent on these performances; in fact, my business life did not suffer at all from the little time that these projects required. However, I did begin to suffer new reverses in business. Every investment became unbelievably unprofitable. I could bet on a *sure* thing and yet lose. Determination to show Melva that I had everything under control drove me to make some foolish moves. I was desperate to show her that I could handle these affairs and be eminently successful as I had been in the past. To say the least, it was very annoying to see Melva's prophecy coming true as one venture after another failed.

Then in 1963 we had a particularly serious argument about religion, and the next morning I found a letter from my wife which caused me to realize the desperate and lonely situation that confronted Melva. She had gone as far as she could go without her husband. The letter truly touched me, and at this time I realized something serious had to be done. It was at this point that I began to accompany my family to Sunday School regularly and to study the scriptures and the writings of Church leaders. We invited the missionaries to dinner often, but still I was not really opening my heart to their message.

In studying the scriptures I discovered new and profound meanings. Especially was I amazed at how the Book of Mormon and Doctrine and Covenants supplement and add veracity to the Bible. Then in class on Sunday I began to feel a radiant spirit among some of the members, and my curiosity began to grow. Now gospel discussions were more common in my life, and soon it was apparent to me that the Book of Mormon was at least unique and exceptionally interesting.

While reflecting on all of this late one night, I realized that I was experiencing that same feeling from within that had been part of me that night in 1956 when I addressed the missionaries in Chicago, and then again in 1960 while discussing the Church with an intelligent friend. Now here it was again, and I knew for certain that the Book of Mormon was what it purported to be, and that therefore everything else must also fall into place. It was a thrilling moment.

I woke Melva, it being about two-thirty in the morning, and we assumed what for me was a very foreign position—we knelt in prayer. While praying, we both experienced a deep feeling of peace and assurance that all would be well in the future. Afterwards I told Melva that I wanted to be baptized—but could I live the covenants, especially in the area of "kindergarten" called the Word of Wisdom? This was now May, 1964, and in an interview I set my baptism for the last Saturday in July. In retrospect, it is foolish that I chose to delay baptism for two months, since I knew the Church was true and I had made up my mind to live by its tenets. I could as easily have set the date for one month or even one week later. The course I followed was a very dangerous one, and I would not recommend it to anyone.

Now the torture began in earnest, and up to the last night prior to baptism, I could not seem to live the Word of Wisdom. We were out to dinner with clients, and I had martinis before dinner, wine with dinner, and a stinger after dinner. I remember I had a couple of drinks at intermission during the show we attended, and then left to catch the 12:04 a.m. train to Scarsdale. We got to Grand Central Station with about ten minutes to spare, so I took Melva into one of my favorite bars and I had two fast drinks. As I took my last puff on the cigarette I was smoking, it was four minutes before twelve and I knew *this was it!* Could I make it? Did I have a real testimony? I had no *doubts* about the Church, but did *I* have sufficient strength?

I determined to stay strong through Saturday; and then Sunday, being the Sabbath, would have to be observed. A doctor friend had given me some pills to help through the coming weeks, and I was armed for the battle.

After coming out of the waters of baptism, I had that exhilarating feeling that comes when the spirit has subjugated the physical man. It was so strong that I knew I had been "hired" by the Lord for his purposes and that I was truly different from what I had been the day before. Since I did not want to be "fired" from the Lord's employ, and since the priesthood was more important to me than any job I had ever had, I knew that the Lord and I would overcome my Word of Wisdom problem, so instead of pills I turned to prayer. Whereas I had been accustomed to having a fresh cigarette in my hand every fifteen minutes, it now became a matter of a prayer on my lips almost every fifteen minutes. I will not detail the conquering of this habit—this minor requirement of gospel living—except to say that it was not easy. But I knew it was necessary, and ever since the day I was baptized, I have been able to testify to the truth of the Word of Wisdom, for I am still in better health than ever before, and the liver and lung impairments, while not cured, are surely arrested.

My father, being a doctor, is amazed at the improvement in me. He is a world-renowned doctor of internal medicine. Recognized as an innovator both in research and in treatment, he was Professor of Gastroenterology at Northwestern University School of Medicine and later was president of the national organization. He has been director of research for the World Medical Association, and has other honors too numerous to detail here. We were a family dedicated to achievement in the world, and were far removed from theology or theological issues.

Dad was pleased that my health improved after my baptism, yet any attempt to discuss the Church created an argument or disagreement. This finally prompted him to tell Melva that she must see to it that I stopped talking religion in front of him.

After six months in the Church, Melva and I were called on a stake mission for two years. This became another milestone in our lives, for we soon discovered that we had neither the desire nor the time to make money; so around April of 1965, we completely stopped working and made our mission a full-time mission. Now with our door open to the missionaries and a prayer that we might be of service to them in their efforts, we began to get calls to talk to investigators. Soon we were talking in sacrament meetings throughout our stake, and during the week we would be with the missionaries, with our own investigators, and opening our home for missionary meetings.

By 1967 we were presenting our program in wards and branches, stakes and districts, and by the end of that year we had completed assignments from Massachusetts to California with many stops in between. This was a labor of love, and we were constantly adding to and changing our format to meet the needs of the group concerned. Our mission was extended by six months, and when it ended, we discovered that we were busier than ever. By the end of 1969, we looked back and found that we had criss-crossed the United States by car alone (not counting air travel) almost twenty times since 1965, had accumulated over 120,000 miles of missionary travel, appeared in over a hundred different wards and branches, and had seen the Church in action throughout the nation. Although an exact total is not available, we have had the privilege of giving over six hundred separate presentations with music and the spoken word.

In all this we received much more than we could ever have given. What a testimony it was to us! We found the Church to be the same in the East or the West, for everywhere the saints are striving for the same goal—eternal exaltation. To us, The Church of Jesus Christ of Latter-day Saints is a living miracle. Where else in the world will you find an organized religion, association, or group of any type that has so many people unselfishly committed to the same objectives?

It is interesting to reflect upon the way the gospel changes one's life. Among other blessings, since the day I was baptized Melva and I have not been separated for more than a day; and we work, play, and pray together in all things. Our lives have become totally inseparable both personally and professionally, and—contrary to the "old days"—we never have a conflict of interests. In fact, we love this great blessing of togetherness and are grateful for it. We have discovered that for life to have real meaning, it must give real service. Now we are happily rebuilding our lives, asking only that the Lord's will be done.

One day Melva and I sat reflecting on our blessings and the great opportunities we have to be of service to our Father in heaven. At the time we were with Melva's mother. We were expressing wonderment that the missionaries ever found us, when Melva's mother humbly admitted that she had sent them to our home.

Melva's mother was born to Mormon parents who both died when she was a child. She was raised by relatives, married while young, moved to California, divorced her husband, and married again out of the Church. (Her daughter, Melva, never knew about the Church until years later, when she learned of it in the way I have recounted.) My mother-in-law reactivated herself after a series of personal tragedies and, unknown to us, committed herself to the gospel. She then sent the light of the gospel into her daughter's life, thus benefiting me and my family and my brother and his children—and so on it will go, particularly as we do our genealogical and our missionary work.

We are truly grateful for the adversities in our lives, and we know that if they had not come we would not have the gospel to enjoy as we do today. We are blessed by the whisperings of the Holy Ghost, which tell us that God lives, that Jesus is the Christ, that Joseph Smith was a great prophet, and that there is a prophet at the head of the Church today. We know that the Book of Mormon is the work of God. Melva and I pray that we may be worthy servants in the Lord's kingdom and that we may endure to the end.

DON VINCENZO DI FRANCESCA

FORTY-YEAR WAIT FOR BAPTISM

This story spans an ocean and a lifetime. It takes the participant from his native Sicily to America, where he obtains a degree as pastor. More important, in a trash pile he finds a precious book of scripture. The book lacks only one thing—identification. It is without cover or title page.

The thrilling contents of the book now inspired Don Vincenzo's life and supplemented his sermons. But the ministerial reaction was the classic one—this must be heresy because it is not in the Bible. Don Vincenzo, however, had received the Spirit's witness that the book was true, and he would not retract. His account of the "trial" he received and his firm defense of the book without a name could almost make one think that a modern Luther was facing his accusers.

It took twenty years to discover the name and publisher of this precious book—the Book of Mormon—and another twenty before the eager convert could receive baptism. All that time Don Vincenzo was without Church association. The reader may well ponder whether his own faith would have stood that test.

Brother Di Francesca died firm in the faith in 1966. At his request, his story is dedicated to the Italian Mission.

Leaving the waters of the Mediterranean Sea on the north coast of Sicily about 80 kilometers east of Palermo, one can make his way up the steep slopes of the Madoni mountain range and eventually reach several small Sicilian villages, typically situated on the crests of the highest peaks. Passing through Santo Gibilmanna one travels several more kilometers to the tiny city of Gratteri. This was where on September 23, 1888, at 9:00 a.m., Don Vincenzo Di Francesca was born and where on November 18, 1966, he passed from this life.

Many citizens of this tiny village experience birth, life, and death while never venturing more than twenty or thirty kilometers from their homes in all their lives. This might have been the lot of Vincenzo had not a sequence of events led him far away and eventually brought him to a knowledge and acceptance of the gospel of Jesus Christ.

From his very early years, Vincenzo was religiously inclined. After his elementary education was complete, his grandfather Antonine arranged for him to receive private religious training from the older man's cousin, Vincent Serio, who unfolded the Old and New Testaments to the lad. Vincenzo was so successful in all the lessons that his tutor praised him with the words: "Thou art blessed."

At the age of twelve Vincenzo was admitted to the Gymnasium Lay-Clerical where he studied religion for four-and-a-half more years.

His brother Antonine, who was then residing in New York City, invited Vincenzo to spend his seminary vacation in America, and he accordingly left Naples on a steamship. In New York he struck a fast friendship with his brother's friend, a Methodist pastor of the Italian Branch Chapel. Soon Vincenzo became a teacher of that congregation, and because of the merit of his teaching it was proposed that he take the Evangelical course of both Old and New Testament, at Knox College of New York, where he got his degree as pastor in November 1909.

Early one cold morning Vincenzo received a note about a sick friend. While he was on his way down Broadway toward the ailing friend's home, a strong breeze from the open sea rustled the pages of a book which had been thrown upon a barrel full of ashes ready for the city trash truck. The form and the binding of the pages gave him the idea that it was a discarded religious book, and curiosity pushed him to retrieve it. He plucked it from the ashes and beat it against the trunk of the trash barrel. He looked at the frontispiece and found it torn; the cover was completely missing. The fury of the wind turned the pages in his hand, and he saw names that he had never in his life seen before. In his haste to go on to his destination, he wrapped the soiled book in the newspaper he had just bought and continued toward his colleague's house, where he visited with him and consoled and advised him.

After Vincenzo's return home, as soon as he could get his coat off and warm himself, he opened the book and began to read. He came across some of the writings of Isaiah—a name he recognized—and was convinced that it was a fine religious book he had found. But he could not detect the name of it since the cover and some pages were missing, and other pages were too soiled to be legible. He went out to the drug store and bought 20 cents' worth of denatured alcohol, and with this and a cotton-pad he washed the remainder of the pages. Then he read them.

"I felt as though I was receiving fresh revelation and much new light and knowledge," he recalls. "I was also charmed to think of the source by which I had obtained the book. Many of the lectures in the book left in my memory a strong magnetic attraction, and I felt urged to re-read it several times, always satisfied that it fit very well with other scripture, as though it were a fifth Gospel of the Redeemer.

"The next day I locked my door and knelt with the book in my hands. First, I reviewed the 10th chapter of Moroni, and then I prayed to know if the book were of God. I also asked if I could mix the words of it with the four Gospels of Matthew, Mark, Luke, and John in my public preaching.

"While I was in that pose, awaiting a positive answer, I first felt my body become cold and my heart palpitate as if it would speak, and then I felt a gladness as if I had found something of extraordinary preciousness. It left in my memory sweet consolation and supreme joy that human language finds no words to describe.

"The book was easy to understand without effort. The more I read it and thought about it, the more I was impressed that I had received the assurance that God had answered my prayer and I knew that the book was of great benefit to me and to all who would heed its words.

"Within a few days my preaching was strung with the new words of the book, and the listeners became amazed and enthralled with the new power in these sermons, at the same time becoming indifferent to some of my fellow preachers. Thus while the esteem towards me grew, so did professional anger and envy and suspicion. One day I was interrupted in a meeting by the Vice Venerable, when he heard me talking of Mary the Virgin and substituting the vision of 1 Nephi 11:15-36. This arrogant authority encouraged my colleagues to sit in all my meetings and contradict any new doctrine! These contradictions and indignities made me rebel, and I became disobedient to the warnings for me to observe the strict methods of the sect.

"Next I was denounced to the Committee of Censure who, with fatherly words, counseled me to burn the book of the devil that had brought so much trouble to the harmony of the brothers who loved me.

"I testified to them as follows: 'I find the book precise under every respect to the writings of the prophets, and the words themselves testify that the book is of the God whom we profess to adore. I do not know to what precise church it belongs, but for certain it talks about the appearance of the Redeemer, after his crucifixion, to a remote people organized into a nation upon this continent, and the Redeemer himself there organized a Church with apostles and priesthood like the Church that he organized during his ministry among the Jews; and he gave commandments and laws. The great trouble with most of us is that we do not apply the teachings of the gospel to ourselves. We do not examine ourselves and find out wherein we are failing. Knowledge without practice is like a glass eye—all for show and nothing for use. There is nothing more true than the fact that it is *works* that count. Faith without works is dead, like the body without spirit. It is only a short time after death until we must bury the body. We cannot keep it.

" 'The book that the Committee counsels me to burn talks of a church, but the missing pages do not let me know where it is. It is better, instead of burning the book, that we practice what is in it, because certainly it gives us more light and knowledge and more faith to perform all our works, than the teachings of others. I cannot burn the book, because I fear God and I have asked him if it is true, and my prayer has been answered affirmatively, positively, without a shade of doubt. I feel it in my whole heart, mind, and body at this instant. Neither can I permit its burning, and since you insist on pronouncing the sentence to burn the remaining pages of the book which you say is of the devil, I tell you that it is the devil who suggests to you to persist in your decision in order to bring you into perdition as Judas Iscariot was, who sold the Redeemer for thirty pieces of silver. I am encouraged to tell you in this instant that your eyes are of glass and that you are all near to God with your words but far from him with your hearts and your works!'

"That was as the fire to the powder in the gun. The Committee got up and cried, 'It is enough! That book, which oppresses you, must be burned or you will incur the most serious displeasure.'

"I replied, 'I repeat, I will not burn the book. I prefer to go out of the ministry rather than burn the book!'

"In April of 1914, this heavy conflict had its conclusion before the Council of Peace of the sect, and I was invited to a conciliation. But I found that the subject of the judgment was not being changed. The Vice Venerable started the interrogation with affable manners, believing that my unyielding attitude had been provoked by the sharp rap administered by the members of the Committee of Discipline. He spoke with much benevolence, and then stated, 'You must be noble enough to burn that vessel of falsehoods that has brought bitterness to the Brothers of the Good Shepherd!'

"I replied, 'The musicians have changed, but the music is the same, namely that I must destroy the book with fire without anyone examining its contents. If I burn the book I offend the Godhead.'

"I was given one last warning: 'Repent of your stubbornness!'

" 'No.' I stood with the contested book in my hands, listening to the words of the Judge stripping me of my degree of Pastor and of every right and privilege in the Church of the Good Shepherd.

"I left with fresh self-confidence at having defended my cause and that of the book of unknown name.

"On May 15, 1914, the Supreme Synod examined a list of member petitioners and reviewed my case of disobedience. They called upon me to be judicious and to abandon the "infidel book" and repent, as the Synod was of the intention to pardon my stubbornness. I refused, so they confirmed the decision, classed me as an habitual and incorrigible rebel against the ordinances of the religious sect, and pronounced definitely my removal from the body of the church.

"November 26, 1914, the Italian Consulate of New York called me to embark for Italy as a soldier in the 127th Infantry Regiment stationed at Florence, Italy. May, 1915, I was sent to the front. At one point I was seriously censored by the commander of the company on report by the Catholic chaplain who was aware of my loyalty to the book with no cover. I was punished with ten days in a tent with only bread and water, and was told never to tell anyone again about the history of a degraded people that are the American redskins.

"After my discharge in 1919 I returned to the United States, and there I met my old friend Mike, the pastor of the Methodist Church, who knew my preceding history and whom I greatly esteemed. He frankly interceded in my favor, asking that I be readmitted to the congregation as a lay brother, afterwards making steps toward a reconciliation. It was very hard, but at the end, being specific that they were conducting an experiment, they called me to accompany my protector abroad on a mission. We went to Auckland, New Zealand; and then to Sidney, Australia, where I found some Italian emigrants who had serious questions about certain gospel translations in some of the Catholic and Protestant editions of the Bible. They were unsatisfied by my minister friend's answers but, being in possession of the truth, I convinced them. When they wanted to know where I had learned such teachings, I spoke of the book in my possession. It was sweet for them but very bitter for my colleague. At first he bore with me, but I could not resist the strong urge to preach the divine truth, and finally Mike denounced me in his reports. Again the Synod put in force the decision of May 15, 1914, and I was forever out of the Sect.

"In May, 1930, I stumbled onto the source of my precious book. It happened while I was looking in my French dictionary for the significance of a pulley invented by a Frenchman. As I was thumbing through the M's, my eyes fell upon the words "Mormon sect." I quickly wrote to the president of the 'University of Provo,' which was mentioned in the article, and asked for information about the remainder of the book that talks of Nephi, Alma, Mosiah, Mormon, Isaiah, Lamanites, etc. He passed my letter to the President of The Church of Jesus Christ of Latter-day Saints, and in another month I heard from President Heber J. Grant. He sent me a copy of the Book of Mormon in Italian and said that he had informed the president of European Missions in Liverpool, England, Elder John A. Widtsoe, to arrange baptism.

"On June 5, 1932, Elder John A. Widtsoe of the Council of the Twelve came to Naples intending to baptize me, but a revolution between Fascists and anti-Fascists on the Island of Sicily caused the police of Palermo to prevent me from going to Naples, and I had to wait for another chance, like Moses in anticipation of the promised land.

"I was called to arms during the Italian-Ethiopian war in 1934, and this further prevented anyone with authority from reaching me for baptism.

"On January 14, 1937, I started correspondence with Elder Richard R. Lyman, European Missions President, and later with the president of the British Mission. President Hugh B. Brown of that mission eventually came to Rome intending to baptize me, but his letter of invitation for me to go to Rome was delayed until the day in which he and his family left Rome for America because of the outbreak of World War II, when the missionaries in Europe returned to America. Thus I was deprived of baptism, and cut off from any news of the Church.

"I remained a faithful follower and fervent preacher of the gospel of this dispensation, being in possession of the standard works of the Church. I translated those works in my idiom and sent the important chapters to persons of my acquaintance.

"On February 13, 1949, I started again the correspondence with Elder John A. Widtsoe and I asked him to help me to be baptized soon. He answered that he had written asking President Samuel Bringhurst of the Swiss-Austrian Mission to come down to Sicily and baptize me.

"On January 18, 1951, I was baptized by President Bringhurst in the Thermal Waters of Termini Imerese, Sicily, in the South of Italy.

"In 1954 I made a trip to the Swiss Temple for my own endowments, and this first step was quickly followed by other trips to do temple work for my ancestors.

"You can see that I have toiled hard to find the salvation in the kingdom of God which was spoken of in the remainder of the pages of the book without title page or cover. I pray earnestly that my story will be copied into the historical record of the Italian District [now Mission] so that future converts can learn clearly that man does not live by bread alone but lives also by the word of God. To all the saints in Zion I clasp hands across the ocean in true brotherhood."

Brother Francesca's story was supplied by the President of the Italy Mission, Leavitt Christensen.

ALAN CHERRY

A NEGRO'S LIFE CHANGED

The combination of circumstances under which Alan Cherry was converted must set something of a record. To be converted while in military service is not too uncommon an experience but to receive the Spirit's witness as a Negro while in a military confinement facility is surely unusual.

It all began with Alan's growing realization that there is more to life than the pattern of drink, drugs and illicit sex into which he and his Air Force associates had fallen. Casting off this way of life, he began an earnest search for truth through prayer and Bible study.

LDS readers will be both intrigued by the story of how he was nudged in the right direction and inspired by his testimony of the gospel. Of particular note is his faith-promoting, positive approach to the subject of priesthood.

Alan's changed life is reflected in his goals for personal growth and Church service. He finds measurable fulfillment of such goals not only in the usual day-to-day activities but also as a student at Brigham Young University, as part of a BYU show touring the Orient, and as a member of "The Free Agency" group which entertains and inspires the youth of the Church.

A New York negro, I was in the Air Force stationed in Texas. I weighed 235 pounds, and at my short stature I was "chock-full" to say the least. I decided to try an experiment just to prove that I had the necessary willpower to lose weight without the help of special diets.

Successfully going from 235 to 136 pounds in nine months gave me a lot of energy and self-confidence, so much so that I decided to channel my new-found willpower towards solving other personal problems. For some time, I had been pondering over the meaning of life. There were conclusions which I felt I must reach about national riots, the Vietnam war, and other decisions and principles which I'd been considering. I made up my mind not to be a follow-the-crowd type after becoming aware of the degraded level of morality on the base and in town. I had seen some bold-faced acts committed in a very open manner. Now was the time to begin the permanent separation of truth and falsehood in my own mind—I would become a seeker of truth.

During the next few months I read and meditated whenever I could, and by October of 1965, being somewhat frustrated with trying to grasp philosophical principles, I decided to take a brief rest and go home for a while.

I took leave and returned home to New York City, where I found a friend who had become an Orthodox Moslem. She told me about her religion. I listened and I honestly thought about it, but I could not accept what she told me. It did not seem to be the entire truth. My premise was that unless a religion or a philosophy had all the truth—no errors—there was certainly no reason for me to waste my time on something that would lead me only to a portion of the truth. So I figured that if man could somehow get into contact with all of the truth in its vibrancy, he then could attach himself to it and grow and develop, thus escaping falsehood altogether. It's easy to see that many of the world's people aren't evil, but they are just unfortunate in that they have not discovered the truth. I spent only a short time at home, returning to Texas the following week, still determined to "search."

On October 19, 1967, I was called to my first sergeant's office to discuss a minor disciplinary matter. I took the occasion to tell him that I was engrossed in a personal quest for truth and would seek to leave the Air Force if it impeded my development. Because it appeared then that this quest would take all of my time, I foresaw the possibility of future conflict with the Air Force. I told him I realized that I had made a four-year service commitment, but that at the time I made that commitment I had had no idea that this situation would arise. His suggestion was to wait two years—the approximate time remaining on my enlistment—and not consider interrupting my enlistment in this way.

I said in return, "Well, I don't know if I can wait two years. How do I know I can ever get this energy again or get the unity within to go out and seek truth with real determination to find it?" I didn't mean to take the position that I was telling him what the terms of my military enlistment would be; I was simply suggesting there should be some way the Air Force could assist me. I really didn't expect the Air Force to adjust to me, so I was considering leaving it. This could be facilitated if there were some procedures that could lead to a compromise. Therefore, all I was doing was just alerting the sergeant to a possible situation that might arise in the future.

On November 19, 1967, I met him again concerning the same disciplinary matter, and I advised him again of my intentions. His attitude had not changed; he was still angered by my words. By mid-December his views were the same, but I had changed considerably. I had stopped drinking, I had given up smoking cigarettes and marijuana and drinking "cough syrup," and I had become chaste. I did almost nothing but read and think.

I met with my first sergeant again about December 12, 1967, formally to ask for a discharge. He told me the only way I could do this was with the base psychiatrist's recommendation. He then called to schedule an appointment for me with the base psychiatrist, and he told me the appointment was set for early January. I didn't want to wait that long, but I agreed since, according to the first sergeant, that was the earliest opening.

I tried studying the philosophers between our meeting and early January. Admittedly I didn't give them years, just minutes, but none could tell me by their works where truth was. So following any of them seemed a waste of time, because I was interested only in the one who possessed absolute truth. The only name that came to my thoughts at this time whom I hadn't tried was Jesus Christ. So I bought a Bible, realizing I hadn't given him a chance. I had judged the Bible by the people I knew to be Christians and rejected it because of their conduct and their own confusion concerning Christian scripture. I read the New Testament first, wanting to see if I could pick up its spirit; and if I could, then I would be willing to follow Christ's teachings for the rest of my life.

After reading a portion of Matthew, I was convinced that it was true. Every time I would read a verse that was potent, it would just leap out at me, while the parables all seemed to vibrate within me with new meaning. I tried to absorb so much that I couldn't go beyond a few verses without stopping to marvel at its truth. All these years, I thought, I have been fooling around doubting and not understanding. I decided to follow Jesus Christ and his teachings by dedicating myself to his cause, whether he manifested himself to me or not. Moreover, I was determined to seek truth until I had become one with it. I wanted to avoid becoming a sunshine saint in the spiritual sense. I wanted to prove my sincerity and show my level of commitment to Jesus Christ no matter what the consequence.

Needing assistance from my first sergeant, my squadron section leader and the base psychiatrist, but receiving from them what appeared at the time to be indifference, I decided to stop work and put all my time in my new cause. I knew also that I might be transferred, and the possibility of a transfer to a new base bothered me when I considered how a new squadron section leader might react to my situation. I didn't relish the idea of starting all over again with new personnel. I was even more prompted to make my stand by stopping work when I considered this prospect. Perhaps my judgment was bad, but with the limited understanding I had at the time, this seemed the only course.

On January 19, 1968, the inevitable happened. I was apprehended and placed in the base confinement facility when I disobeyed a lieutenant's order to go to work. I had spent about three to four weeks in confinement when I found out that if I hadn't disobeyed that order, I probably would have received an administrative discharge. Although I was inwardly unhappy when I disobeyed the order to go to work, I did have confidence that I had the courage to follow through to conclusion in a crisis situation. This knowledge had come to me in the weight-losing episode.

Moreover, I had submitted a request for a discharge while I was in confinement and I expected to be free soon to resume my quest. So even if the world would consider this a mark against me and they were right in so doing, at least I knew I was honest in making that mistake. Although depressed that February, I reasoned that if I could function within some truth-seeking organization I would be ten times more effective than in the Air Force. Of course if everyone felt this way, the United States would be in a very serious position. At that time I did not appreciate that all young men have the responsibility to serve in the armed forces regardless of the inconvenience or their personal desires.

Worried because of my ability to make mistakes, I thought participation in an organization would make my truth-seeking efforts more exact. But what organization was there? There was Catholicism and there was Protestantism, but neither satisfied me. I couldn't really cite any definite objections, but I also could not feel right about them.

One day about mid-February, while I was still in the confinement facility, I noticed in the library for the first time a pamphlet entitled, "Which Church is Right?" I looked at it and saw the author's name, "Mark E. Petersen." I had heard of religious writers being called Doctor, Reverend, Bishop, and a number of other titles, and I was skeptical of this man's authority on the subject of truth because he had no title. But deciding that I wasn't being fair to him, I gave in and read the pamphlet. I was very pleased with the text; it didn't tear down other religions, but just simply explained what Mormonism had to offer. But when I had finished it, it just sort of ended. It explained what Mormonism was founded upon, but not "Where do I go from here?" and "Whom do I contact?" However, I noticed that the pamphlet said something about Joseph Smith's testimony—that Mormonism was based upon it. So I again turned to the bookshelf and saw there another pamphlet, "Joseph Smith Tells His Own Story." I picked it up and read it. That's when it all happened—the true awakening.

As I read the testimony, I felt as if I had a forest fire within me. Up until then I had thought: "Well, I'm a fool. I have made a mistake." I was getting weak as every day progressed, because I was not only just trying to seek truth, I was trying to be totally objective about it, realizing that if I was wrong I would be my worst enemy and first critic. And I wanted to completely make an honest confession. I didn't want to slip, dodge, or hide.

Now, as I read Joseph Smith's story I saw that he was misunderstood also, and I thought that it's funny how people just won't believe what you say when you seem to be in an obscure position, different, "peculiar." Well, when I had read Joseph Smith's story, I thought: "It's good; I like it. But unless God puts his stamp on it I can't really accept it, because then I won't know whether I've accepted something that has that grain of error or whether it's all true." So I turned the pamphlet over—and there were the words from Moroni 10:4.

It was just like a gulp in my throat. Boy! I thought, it says it right here—just ask God. And this is what I had wanted, because if I had had to ask another man about the truthfulness of the gospel, whether it was truly of God or of man, I would have been inclined to question the doctrine here and there because I would have had no assurance that it was the true religion. So I decided to pray about it; I decided to ask God whether Joseph Smith's testimony was true. I knew I should have read the Book of Mormon first, but I didn't have a copy, and I just couldn't wait.

At this point I made my big error. Somehow I misinterpreted Moroni 10:4 and assumed that an *angel* would come and visit *me* and give me a knowledge of the truth of this pamphlet and then the truth of the gospel. I supposed that manifestations could happen on a clear day and people who would observe might mistake them for just another daily occurrence or even not be aware of it when really something rare and marvelous had happened. But I knew that if an angel brighter than the noon-day sun should come in that confinement cell, it would cause considerable commotion. I did wonder if this was the correct approach, but I figured, Well, I'll go ahead anyway; so I determined to go ahead and ask for an angel!

That night, when I was alone, I sat down on the floor of my cell and folded my arms. I was out of sight so that the sergeant on guard duty could not see me. As I bowed my head, I began to think of my past. I started to cry. I'd cried before, but these were new, very humble tears. There were tears for all my sins I had committed, all my weaknesses, the times I had taken the Lord's name in vain, mocked Christ, cracked jokes and made ugly expressions about God and Christ.

I began to pray. I told my Heavenly Father in tears that I was now trying my best to be pure, to obey the commandments, and I admitted that it was really a strain on me to do it. I admitted that I was worth nothing in comparison with Christ, and after all I had done I was not worthy to meet them face to face. Yet I knew that by grace I was permitted to ask for a testimony. I asked Heavenly Father to let me know if Joseph Smith's testimony was true.

I prayed with my eyes closed, and as the words came out of my mouth in a fumbling manner and the tears streamed down my face, I became definitely aware that I was not alone. I felt as if my head was pointed down to my left and I couldn't raise it; I wanted to look, but I didn't feel worthy enough. But I believe I was seeing spiritually—that feeling so intense that it's almost like seeing. I had this feeling intensely within that my soul was being turned around and examined for its relative worth. The feeling, though pleasurable, grew so intense that I was shocked and startled.

I stopped praying. I opened my eyes and shook myself to gain my composure. At that very instant I could no longer feel the presence nor feel the sensation with me.

It wasn't long after that night that I realized the confusion I felt as a result of this experience was a conflict between what I had made up my mind beforehand was going to happen and being able to understand what really did happen. For so long I had dwelt on the scriptures from John where Christ states that those who keep his commandments and love him will be loved of the Father, and in conclusion states, "I will love him, and will manifest myself to him." My anticipations were based entirely upon this scripture and were greatly reinforced by Joseph Smith's experience. However, not being aware of the nature of the spirit, I had made up my mind to receive an experience directly through my physical senses, more specifically through sight and sound. Had

I been more spiritually prepared, had my mind been more spiritually oriented, I would have been able to understand the nature of the experience much better.

After that night I began to pray every day that God might somehow permit me to have a clarification of that first experience. I wanted something that related to me specifically, that I knew was true, that I could believe in. It wasn't long until this prayer was answered in a manner least expected.

I still didn't have a Book of Mormon. On February 22, 1968, I met my first Mormon, who was brought into confinement for drunk and disorderly conduct. Right away I realized that not only was he the answer to my prayers, but that there is no magic potion given a Mormon that makes him a better person. Previously I had thought that possibly when you take upon yourself the new and right and unique relationship with God, you get a power that lifts you ten steps above everyone else, and progression from then on is unceasing. Now I realized that this thing about working out your salvation is literal. You have to "cut the mustard" day after day, and growth is an achievement, not a gift. So when I saw that Mormon, I gained more compassion; I gained more love and understanding. That young Mormon did some beautiful things for me. He had me write to his aunt, and she wrote to the Texas Mission president, who in turn sent out the missionaries. He also brought me a copy of the *Reader's Digest* about a week after our first meeting, and showed me the article about the Church in the February, 1967 issue. It said that all male members can have the priesthood at twelve years of age—except Negroes, who can't have it at all.

From the start I realized that this doctrine was true, and I accepted it. I thought: "Well, I know that the things that have happened in the past four or five months—the manifestation, the Mormon friend, and the events leading up to them—came to me from Heavenly Father; for each, the testimony came through the Spirit and not through my own mind. I can feel it with my heart more than I can reason it out with my mind. So, if God has spoken to me, who am I to challenge his word just because it may appear as error to other men? I know that most men exist on this earth by the improper use of pride, power, prominence, and position. These things mean as much to them as does the word of God— sometimes more. So they would probably reject this doctrine of priesthood restriction because of their inability to understand it by mental reasoning." I also thought that a black man's first reaction usually would be to deny the possibility that this doctrine is true because it seems to take a prejudicial stand against him and to deny him something he should have.

But I knew that I had stepped away from the world and sought God, and that he had spoken to me through the Spirit. So how could I dare come back and say to him: "This doctrine is wrong. I won't join your church because I can't have a particular position to which I aspire." Somehow it didn't seem that this attitude would be consistent with the doctrine Christ taught—that he who would be greatest in the kingdom of heaven should be the servant of all. If the greatest man, the Lord himself, would stoop down and wash his disciples' feet and show through serving what true greatness was—the power of love—then I did not need position or prominence or pride in order to serve.

I knew what would come; I knew people wouldn't be able to understand. But I knew, too, that I had my ability as a child of God to be creative, to use my unlimited, untapped power. If I had asked someone when I was heavy, "Do you believe I can lose a hundred pounds in seven months?" he probably would have said, "I doubt it." When I did accomplish the feat, many people were flabbergasted. So I thought, if I can channel into my living of the gospel the same willpower and dedication I applied to losing weight, I can make not having the priesthood be a beautiful thing. In living that way I can help some priesthood holders to realize that it's the Spirit of the Lord energizing the priesthood that makes it really function in the superlative way. It was clear, too, that if I could have spiritual impressions, if I could have good ideas, if I could have the spirit of the Lord, then I could work out my salvation whether I held the priesthood or not. The parable of the talents clearly illustrates that whatever talent you do have, you are expected to develop it and bring it into use for the benefit of all mankind. It didn't matter to me essentially who led or who followed, just that the job which had to be done was done.

So, I was determined to capture the big idea, the image of what the gospel is all about, and spread the good news and share it with everyone with whom I come in contact by using my creativity to do it. I decided to leave the service and to devote my life to tapping that creativity.

The Apostle Paul had impressed me greatly with his missionary work as I had read the scriptures. In turn I decided that this would really be how to enjoy the gospel in the spiritual sense—go out and in some way sow missionary seeds, find some medium of expression which would convert people. So at no time was I worried or concerned about not being able to rise through the echelons of the priesthood, for though I didn't have that power, I had my hands full with this new task of just trying to share what I had learned through the Spirit, through that feeling which is as intense sometimes as visual seeing. I had received a testimony of the truth, a knowledge of it, and it had changed my life, made every day beautiful, made my horizons greater than I had ever dreamed possible.

After receiving a rejection of my discharge request, I was court martialed on March 1, 1968.

I received a letter from the missionaries about April 13th, and I met them about the 18th and had a preliminary discussion with them. I had my first lesson about the 25th of April. On April 26th I was surprised when I was released from confinement because my bad conduct discharge had been disapproved by higher authority. I knew that this, too, was a subtle work of the hand of God, simply because it was very unlikely that officers in a higher court would really give so much attention to such an "open and shut case" involving an obscure person like myself. That day I gave much thanks to Heavenly Father, for though things had been very bleak, I could see that it was the Lord's hand that saved me.

I received the remaining five missionary lessons in the next ten days, and I was baptized on May 9, 1968, at the Abilene Branch. On May 24th I received my discharge from the service and decided to return home to New York City primarily for three reasons: to go about the task of making some definite contribution to the Church, to share the gospel with my family, and to try to do something to bring this truth to all black people.

F. Enzio Busche

LIFE'S QUESTIONS ANSWERED

With Hitler's vaunted Third Reich tumbling in battered ruins in 1945, Germany called on boys to fill gaps in her beleaguered army. One of these was fourteen-year-old Enzio Busche.

In a U. S. prisoner-of-war camp, young Enzio experienced the desolate feeling that home and all that had seemed certain was now gone forever. Yearnings to find himself took hold. Ten years later a personal miracle drew from him the commitment of dedication to understand and serve the God who had healed him.

His intensified search for truth and the way to serve was rewarded by LDS missionaries being led to his door. Brother Busche has honored the commitment he made in his youth by diligent activity in God's kingdom, where he now serves as regional representative to the Twelve for Germany.

———————

I was born in pre-war Germany, the son of a businessman who built up a large printing concern through his careful diligence. Being born at that time and place meant experiencing childhood under the Hitler regime, a strict political order which directed and controlled all phases of life. I saw all sides of World War II and especially in the last year, I experienced the fate of those whose health and life were constantly in danger. I saw my home completely destroyed, and experienced the chaos of beaten and starving postwar Germany.

The last few months of the war I spent as a German soldier, although I was only fourteen years old. Later, in an American prisoner-of-war camp, I first realized that the home I had known and the future that had once seemed so certain were gone, and that I had to begin a new life. A deep, indescribable yearning took hold of me. Like most people at that time, I longed to find myself. Who am I? Is this all there is to life? What is to become of me? I searched for God and for reasons for all that I had seen and experienced. But regrettably, everyday life and the need of bare necessities absorbed nearly my full attention. A year later, when I finally went back to school, after all the death and chaos, it seemed an absurd and trivial act to study Latin vocables as though nothing had happened.

Life went on. Questions went unanswered. I tried like most people to avoid thinking deeply, for there were many uncomfortable and apparently unanswerable questions.

In 1955, I was hit hard by an incurable liver ailment. Nothing was said to me about my not recovering, but I felt that the time had come which I knew must eventually come to everyone. Yet I was only in my early twenties, and I hoped against fate. My father stood by my bedside, believing I would die in a matter of days.

The unanswered questions of my life and the resulting uncertainty were filling my soul with panic and fear. My soul was weighed down by feelings of guilt and responsibility. It seemed as if there were no way out. As I felt the end nearing, something from within me said, "If you pray now, you will regain your health." I was able to say a prayer, perhaps the greatest that a person in that situation can pray: *"Thy will be done."*

In the instant that I spoke that prayer, I felt a strength outside myself change me and fill me with certainty that I would be well. A shining, positive joy took hold of me, and I promised myself that I would never forget or deny that experience or the knowledge that I had gained from it. I committed myself to seek a conscious life of dedication to understanding and serving the God or power that had healed and changed me.

My sudden improvement was considered a miracle by the doctors, but my father insisted that they perform an exploratory operation. Everyone was amazed when the surgeon found a new liver like a baby's, with nothing wrong, without scars from my ailment. For months afterward, I could eat only baby food because of my new liver.

Soon I could read, and while convalescing I read the Bible from Genesis through Revelation, interrupting my study only to eat and sleep. This gave me the certainty that we are children of a Heavenly Father, who purposely sent us to earth for our own good. I understood the law of free agency—that we may decide either to become like our Father and remain his children eternally, or to be overcome by other powers to our own distress and damnation. I realized that it was Jesus Christ, the Redeemer of man, who had shown me the way in my time of need.

After regaining my health, I had but one goal—to discover whether or not the Church of Christ was on the earth, and if so, to find it. I knew that there were hundreds of churches and that it would be hopeless to attempt to investigate them all individually.

I began by attending, for the first time with full conscious intent, the Protestant church to which my family belonged. I went to the pastor and told him of my experience and of my new willingness to help. He could not hide his great surprise. His first reaction was to suggest that I visit a psychiatrist. This was a real shock, and I had the feeling that this man had little in common with the servants of God described in the scriptures. I forgave him, visited church functions, and did all that a lay member of that church can do. I tried to lead an honest life, and prayed daily with my wife. I promised myself that I would sooner die than forget the great experience I had and what I had learned.

A couple of weeks later, the pastor came and apologized and and asked that I help with a project to visit all members and leave a message with them for him. Glad for the opportunity, I felt I was finally in a position to prove my conviction through action. I soon saw that my message was not making a great impression and that I could not answer many of the questions which were asked about the church that I represented. At my suggestion, all "visiting members" met with the pastor to discuss the Protestant faith. I was disappointed and discouraged to realize after this meeting how few of us really had a testimony of Jesus Christ, the Savior of the world, even though it was preached every Sunday.

At this time, my wife and I decided to kneel and ask God to show us whether or not there were authorized servants of his Son's Church on the earth, and to lead us to them.

A short time later, two young missionaries of The Church of Jesus Christ of Latter-day Saints stood on our doorstep and gave us their message. All that they said seemed strange, unbelievable, almost absurd. But the appearance, attitude, and personality of those young men so impressed me that I invited them to return often.

But in the meantime, since the position of my own church was unclear to me, I went to my church leaders to arrange a discussion between the two groups. A few days later, we of my former church met with four elders of The Church of Jesus Christ of Latter-day Saints, two of whom could not yet understand my native tongue. For me as a critical observer, the hour was an outstanding experience. I saw that the specialist invited by our pastor was unable to speak without anger and hatred. Twice during the evening he became so irritated by the quiet, clear, loving patience of the missionaries that he fully lost his self-control and could add no more to the conversation than outrage.

I made my decision: now was the time for me to earnestly and persistently investigate the message and the power which came from these strangers. If it were the power of God, I would not deny it.

The following weeks were filled with study and prayer. I discovered, to my great joy, the development of the same certainty which came with the prayer at my time of sickness. I knew that God was in control, and that I was progressing in the right direction.

About one-and-a-half years after first meeting with the missionaries, my wife and I were baptized. Our life has changed completely. We are joyful and thankful for every day that we live. Our one wish is to help share this light and knowledge with all people on earth, that their souls may be full of peace, certainty, justice, and truth, and that the catastrophic results of ungodly actions may come to an end.

Our hearts are full of thankfulness for all those who, through their diligence, sacrifice, and testimony, helped bring us the answers to all of life's major questions. We know, with all certainty, that God is our Heavenly Father, that Jesus Christ is his Son, and that his Church in all its power and glory has been restored.

JOHN F. HEIDENREICH

THE GOSPEL TRANSFORMS A MINISTER'S LIFE

For no one is it easy to make the radical change in a way of life which is required by conversion to the gospel. It is doubly difficult for a minister, since the change then involves not only loss of livelihood but also an admission of the inadequacy of his previous faith and teaching and therefore of his life's work up to that point.

When the gospel found John Heidenreich he was a successful and happy Congregational minister in Buffalo, New York. While he had had Church contacts before, had visited Temple Square in Salt Lake City, and had even read the Book of Mormon, he had not been impressed with the Church as a Christian society. This attitude changed in the course of several months mainly through the conversion and testimony of his teen-age son, to whom he gratefully acknowledges his great debt.

Today Brother Heidenreich continues to repay that debt at least partially by his service in the Church and especially by the guidance and teaching he gives to youth as principal of a seminary in Salt Lake City.

———————

My introduction to the Mormons came when I was pastor of The First Congregational Church at Riverhead, Long Island, New York, about 1950. Fay Perkins with two of her children moved into our community from Murtaugh, Idaho. She was of the Mormon faith but began attending our Congregational Church; she explained that the nearest branch of her church was about sixty miles distance from Riverhead and that she was able to attend her sacrament meeting only occasionally. She asked that she might be a member of our congregation. She said she would not join our church as she was a Mormon, but she would be pleased to attend our worship services and contribute. She was warmly accepted and we came to love her dearly. She was one of God's choicest daughters and a fine ambassador for her church. We learned much of the history and some of the standards of Mormonism from this fine woman who became a cherished friend of our family.

My first direct contact with The Church of Jesus Christ of Latter-day Saints came in June of 1952. I had been chosen by our New York Conference as a delegate to the General Council of Congregational Christian Churches meeting that summer in Pomona, California. En route to this meeting, I went with my son, Paul, to Salt Lake City. We registered at a small motel near Temple Square on a Saturday morning. The next morning we attended the broadcast of the Mormon Tabernacle Choir and "The Spoken Word." After the broadcast, a conference of the Mutual Improvement Association was in session; we also attended this meeting.

On that Sunday the tabernacle was packed. Even the entranceways were filled with people who could not get into the building. There was a chain across each doorway keeping any more people from entering. I later told my congregation that this was the first time I ever saw people chained out of church. I was tremendously impressed with the quality of the program presented that morning, with the wholesomeness of the youth who took part, and with the spiritual impact of the meeting. I had never seen a meeting like it before. It touched me deeply.

When I returned to Long Island that summer after the conference in California, I told my wife that I had been to the greatest meeting I had ever attended and that it wasn't in California but in Utah! I told her about the great MIA program of the Mormon Church. She expressed a desire to come to Utah sometime on one of our summer vacations.

The next summer, 1953, we came to Utah with a young physician and his wife who were active in our church. They were British people and had never seen our great West. They proposed the idea that we take our vacation with them and tour the West. We were not sure we could go; such a trip would be a strain on the family economy. One day Mrs. Taylor, the doctor's wife, came to the parsonage and told us to make our plans for the trip. They had just bought a new Chrysler, and she informed us that we were going on this trip at her expense. We knew then that we were going; Mrs. Taylor was the great-granddaughter of Isaac Singer and had inherited a fortune in sewing machine stock.

We came again to Temple Square, where the doctor acquired two missionary copies of the Book of Mormon. He asked me, "What do you know about this book?" I replied that I knew practically nothing about it.

He asked, "How does it come that you are a clergyman and know nothing about this book?" I told him that I had not been able to master all the religious literature in the world.

He replied, "Yes, but you are an American and this book is American. You should be familiar with your own ancient American cultures if you are an educated man."

I had been properly rebuked; I began reading the book. My first impression of the Book of Mormon was that it was a poor imitation of the Bible and probably a forgery. I later had to revise my judgment and entirely reverse myself after a more careful reading of the book.

Dr. Taylor found the Book of Mormon fascinating, and we talked about it frequently as we traveled together that summer. When he wanted to bring up the subject of the Book of Mormon, he would say, "Well, let's get going on the Gold Plate Special." This was my introduction to a book that was to change my life.

Our visit to Temple Square that summer made its impression. We had taken the tour on the temple grounds and had met some spiritually dynamic people. Our interest in the Mormons greatly increased with this visit.

From 1953 to 1958 we had no contact at all with Mormon people. During most of this time, we were busily engaged in a church building project in Buffalo, New York, where I had taken a pastorate. We had worked hard and had much satisfaction in the growth of the congregation and in the completion of a new educational building that was added to the church. The name of our church in Buffalo was the Eggertsville Community Church (Congregational); it was a small church with much vigor. We came to love the people of that church very much. After the new educational building was completed and dedicated, the people of the parish urged us to take a restful vacation. I said to my wife, "Let's go back to Temple Square. It's the most peaceful place I have ever been to."

So we went again to Temple Square in August of 1958. That summer I met a man who was a guide on the Square who has influenced my life more than anyone I have ever known outside my own family. His name is Truman Madsen, and he is a professor of philosophy at Brigham Young University. He told me about the restoration of the gospel. I had never heard about this before and the idea made a deep impression on me. I told Brother Madsen at the time that if the gospel hadn't been restored it certainly needed to be restored, considering all the innovations and distortions that had been introduced into the Christian Church since New Testament times.

There was a long distance between someone telling me that the gospel had been restored and my believing that it had been restored. I would have liked to believe such wonderfully good news, but it seemed incredible that such a tremendous event had occurred in history and the world had taken so little note of it.

Up to this time I had gathered the impression in talking to Mormon people that The Church of Jesus Christ of Latter-day Saints was more of an ethical society than a church. Their emphasis on the Word of Wisdom, social welfare, and education had led me to this hasty conclusion. After learning more about the Church, it became clear that there was a very solid theological core in its structure.

Because of the interest we had shown in the Church on our visit to Temple Square in 1958, missionaries called on us in Buffalo that fall. There were four of them in our area. They wanted to give us the first lesson on the Godhead, but we told them we had been out to headquarters and had a basic understanding of their church and did not care to have the lessons. I invited them to meet with me at my church on Thursdays, which was my day off. So each Thursday afternoon they came for a gospel discussion. I looked forward to their coming each week. We also had them frequently at the parsonage. My wife says that we had fifty different missionary elders at our home for meals that winter and spring.

About this time we had a "problem" in our family. He was fifteen. He didn't think highly of our continuing association with the young Mormon missionaries. He had not been enthusiastic about our church, although he had a deeply spiritual nature. One time I told him, "Fred, if I were a butcher, you would have to carry meat. Since I am not a butcher, but a minister, you have to go to church." My logic didn't seem to impress him. After some time, however, he became interested in the missionaries and asked if he might go over to the branch where the Latter-day Saints held their meetings. I told him he had better go, that he might learn something. He usually gave us a report on these meetings at the Sunday dinner table. We thought it was quite amusing at times. He became very defensive in favor of the Latter-day Saints and always, in any comparison, the Congregationalists came off poorly.

I remember one day Fred said to me: "Dad, you should hear them sing. It comes from the heart, not like that phony thing over at your place."

We were quite proud of our music at Eggertsville Community Church. We had Dr. Paul Homer from the Teachers College in Buffalo directing our choir, and we had Victor Dana playing our new organ; we thought he was about the best organist in Buffalo. He had been a church organist for years. Both of these men were professional musicians under salary from our church. We tried to put on a sacred concert every Sunday, but it didn't impress our son.

He had been attending the branch about two months, and he came home one night glowing like a Christmas tree and said he had a testimony.

My wife looked at me and said, "What is that?"

We didn't have the word "testimony" in our church vocabulary. I explained to her that it was an emotional feeling that people get about their religion. I told her that they get happy and get up in their meetings and testify. She didn't think much of the idea. However, there was soon to be a great change in the way our family looked at things.

It is hard for anyone to change his pattern of life, but much easier for the young than the older. We saw a great change come over our son. After he gained his testimony, he changed from being a very negative person to a person with very positive attitudes. His mother and I agreed that whatever had happened to him, it was good.

One day he said to me, "Dad, if you and Mother will go to Palmyra and pray with me in the grove where the Prophet saw his first vision, you will see what I see. You will leave this church and become a member of The Church of Jesus Christ of Latter-day Saints."

At the time it seemed very unlikely that I would ever join another church; I loved my church and had no desire to leave it. But we went to Palmyra and prayed there in the grove on a mild, sunny day in February, 1959. Coming out of the grove I could see how intent our son was in his new-found faith. A fear entered my heart that he was slipping away from us. I responded to this fear in a regrettable manner; I ridiculed the idea of Joseph Smith being a prophet.

I said, "Whoever heard of a prophet by the name of 'Smith'?" My son was offended at the remark and greatly disappointed at my response at coming to the grove. He later told me that he had been impressed in his prayers that if his parents went to the grove in Palmyra they would join the Church.

I must at this point in the story say how much I owe my son, Fred. Had it not been for his strong testimony that impressed me so much, and the encouragement I also received from his mother, I doubt that I would ever have had the courage to make the break from my old life. I am sure he has done more for me than I can ever do for him. My love for him is very great and very special.

At this time I was having many conflicts in my thinking. I had come to a serious consideration of the Book of Mormon. My approach to the book had been very negative up to this time. The book was deeply disturbing to me. I couldn't seem to free myself from the grip it had upon me. By special training and long association, the Bible held a unique place in my esteem, and I could not accept another book to be equal to it in divine authority.

I was fascinated with the Testimony of the Eight Witnesses which appears as part of the introduction to the Book of Mormon. Who were these men who had stood firmly in their testimony to their deaths? I did some research and learned that they were brothers, farmers, and land owners. They were good citizens. They would have been acceptable men on almost any jury. They said that they handled and hefted the plates, and that the plates had the appearance of gold upon which were engraved characters or letters that appeared to be an ancient work.

The thought occurred to me that if there was a possibility that the Book of Mormon was what it claimed to be, it would make a great difference in my life and the life of my family from that time on. It was an important day when I decided to pray about it. I was fully confident that the Lord would give me an answer. He had spoken to me before in times of special need, and I was sure he would speak to me again.

The answer did not come quickly or easily. Several weeks went by. I had expected a yes or no answer, but no answer came. Finally when the Lord did respond to my prayer, I didn't understand what he was saying to me. The Lord did make it clear to me in this matter that my problem was not with the Book of Mormon but with the Bible. This answer from the Lord shocked me. I believed the Bible to be literally true, and I could not comprehend why the Lord questioned my belief in the book from which I had preached during all those years.

I interpreted this disclosure from the Lord as "letting me off the hook" on Mormonism and meaning that I could return to my familiar scriptures and become more proficient in the knowledge and use of them. The Book of Mormon and other Mormon literature was put aside, and I began to re-read the Bible; I read the Old Testament prophets, the letters of Paul, and the Gospels. To my great surprise, I discovered so much new understanding and so many fresh insights into the Bible that it was as if it were a new book.

This experience gave me much joy. It was like a veil being lifted; things that I had never fully understood or that had had very little meaning for me, suddenly became clear and meaningful. Like a revelation, it broke upon my consciousness that it was the

Book of Mormon which was teaching me a true and more complete understanding of the Bible. Through the guidance of the Spirit and the light I gained from the Book of Mormon, I learned more in a few weeks about the Bible than I had learned from all the years of study I had devoted to man-made theologies and ancient languages. So I took up the Book of Mormon with my Bible, and I have read them together since that time; they have become precious companions.

While I was going through this struggle over the Book of Mormon, one night I had a spiritual dream. A spiritual dream is different from other dreams in its vividness and spiritual character. Such an experience had never happened to me before, nor has it happened to me since that time. In Joel we read: "And it shall come to pass afterward, that I will pour out my spirit upon all flesh; and your sons and your daughters shall prophesy, your old men shall dream dreams, your young men shall see visions." (Joel 2:28.) The Lord was certainly pouring out his spirit upon all flesh. These very words from the prophet Joel had been quoted by the Angel Moroni on the night of September 21, 1823, when he appeared to the prophet Joseph Smith.

The dream: I found myself in a large room furnished in a contemporary style. If I should ever see that room again, I would recognize it immediately. Lying on a couch was a man reading a book. The book was held in the man's hand in such a way that it hid his face from my view. Since I was at that time struggling with the Book of Mormon, I was sure that that was the book the man was reading.

I said to him, "Do you believe what you are reading is true?"

He answered, "No, I don't believe it. It's the most fantastic thing I have ever read."

I was annoyed at his answer and also at his rudeness in not rising from the couch or lowering the book from his face. So with some heat in my words, I answered him.

"Well, I believe it's true and I'll tell you why it has to be true."

Then I proceeded to speak the most golden sentence that ever passed my lips as to why the Book of Mormon had to be true. That sentence came straight from the throne of God. I could never have thought of anything so wise and obviously true. This was my answer. I knew then that the Book of Mormon is a genuine record of an ancient people preserved by the hand of God.

I thought that I must memorize the sentence so that I would always remember it. So I went over and over the sentence so that I could retain it in my memory. While I was mentally repeating the sentence, the man on the couch lowered the book from his face, and I saw who it was. It was *me*!

I was so startled that I awakened, and I couldn't remember a word of the Golden Sentence or even what it was like. The dream disturbed my peace of mind for several days. Then one day I was driving down to church, and the meaning of that dream suddenly dawned on me. I believe the Spirit revealed it to me.

Here is the meaning: The man that someday I was to become was talking to the man that I was—that insensitive, unbelieving man lying on the couch. I was disappointed at the loss of the Golden Sentence, but the Spirit gave me assurance that the sentence would be given me when I needed to use it and was worthy to receive it.

Fear entered my heart many times while I was having these experiences. I felt my little world of neat philosophies being smashed. The missionaries had been making their regular weekly visits, discussing the gospel with us. They seemed to be expecting some kind of positive response from us. I felt that a decision would have to be forthcoming. So one day in the spirit of panic I wrote out carefully "Eight Reasons Why I Could Never Be a Mormon." The next time the missionaries came, I presented them with my eight-point decision. They seemed stunned with disappointment and went away crestfallen.

After some days had gone by, I said to my wife, "I sure miss those missionary boys. I could talk to them about the things of God and they understood. When I try to talk to our own church people about spiritual things, they are embarrassed and want to change the subject. They say, "Pastor, that's your department. If you say it is that way, that's the way it is.""

I said to Bernice, "I think I'll phone the missionaries and ask them to come over."

She said, "If you do, we will go through this whole thing again."

"Well," I said, "I'm going to do it anyway," and I did. And sure enough, we were soon going through "the whole thing again."

I began to have the unhappy feeling that time was running out on me as the pastor of the Eggertsville Community Church. One morning as I was reading the Book of Mormon, I came upon these words: ". . . dispute not because ye see not, for ye receive no witness until after the trial of your faith." (Ether 12:6.) It seemed that these words lifted up off the page and came into my consciousness as though the Prophet Moroni had written them especially for me. I knew that soon my faith was to be tested to the limit, and then I would know for a certainty what I desired most to know; I would have what my Mormon friends called a testimony. I was not to have that testimony until my faith had been tried, and I did not know how the trial would come.

This question kept recurring to me: How could I ever leave my church? Had not the Lord called me to be a pastor many years ago? I had never doubted that calling. Had I been mistaken? If The Church of Jesus Christ of Latter-day Saints was the true Church of Christ upon the earth, why had the Lord not called me into that Church? These thoughts left me confused and questioning. One afternoon when I was in my bedroom at prayer, the Lord spoke to me clearly these words: "You can stay in this beautiful garden that you have made, or you can come with me and play for higher stakes."

It is so hard for the uninspired human mind to comprehend the mind of the Lord. I was puzzled. It seemed impossible for the Lord to have spoken such words. My puritan upbringing revolted against the thought of the Lord using the terms of a gambler. It also seemed unlikely that the Lord would mix his metaphors in an English sentence. I thought my senses must be deceiving me. Yet I heard the words as clearly as I ever heard words spoken from human lips.

It occurred to me some days later that the Lord was telling me that there was a great risk involved in my accepting the concept of the restored gospel as taught by The Church of Jesus Christ of Latter-day Saints. I had a choice. I could remain where I was, where I had achieved a ministry helpful to many people, also where I had attained a measure of success and material security; I was doing a work of service and mercy that was acceptable to the Lord. *Or* I could leave it and labor for greater, celestial rewards for myself and my family. Also, there were "higher stakes" of service to others that I could not imagine at that time. (Sometimes the Lord takes things away from us so that he can give us something better—he took away a ministry I loved and gave me a much larger ministry of teaching the gospel to thousands of youth.) But should I prove unfaithful in the higher calling it would be much better if I remained in "the garden" of service where I was.

The Lord did not "gate-crash" my soul. I had the choice. It was an awesome challenge; I stood to lose my soul if I failed. But I had a warm feeling in my heart that the unseen reward was so great that it was worth any risk.

One evening I was turning the pages in the Doctrine and Covenants and I came upon the 109th section, which I had read before and marked for a more careful study. That evening I bathed my soul in that great section. I know of nothing in the Bible or anywhere else more lofty in its concept of the meaning and purpose of the Christian Church. It is a prayer that the Lord gave the Prophet Joseph which he was to offer at the dedication of the Kirtland Temple. That evening it came down upon me with the force of an avalanche that Joseph Smith was in word and deed a prophet of God. Only a prophet could have such rapport with God and have such penetrating insight into what the Church of Jesus Christ should be like upon the earth.

One March evening in 1959, the four missionaries who frequented our home brought with them another young missionary. He said he was a traveling elder. It was this man, Brother Norman MacAllester, whom the Lord sent to give me the final challenge to be baptized and join the Church of Jesus Christ. I came under the influence of the Spirit that was powerfully present in our home that evening. I looked at my wife and my son who were seated there with me, and I made this statement:

"We are going to leave our church. We are going to sell everything we have and move to a Mormon community in the West where I can study more about the restoration of the gospel, because I believe it is true." I couldn't believe what I was saying! I felt as if I wanted to gather up my words and put them in my pocket so they couldn't be heard. It was very hard for me to make this statement. I couldn't say that I wanted to be baptized and join the Church; that was too big a step for me at that time.

Bernice wept. At first I thought she was upset because we were throwing away the only material security that we had. But she was crying for joy. She had wanted to be baptized for some time, but wanted me to make the decision because it affected my livelihood, and she did not want to influence me to make a decision with which I was not in complete accord. During our last visit to Temple Square, Arthur Bishop, a guide on the Square who had been interested in us, had given her the book, *A Marvelous Work and A Wonder*, by LeGrand Richards. She had been convinced of the truthfulness of the restored gospel by this great missionary book. She was always a step ahead of me in our search. Both she and Fred were ready for baptism some time before I was; I had so much theological driftwood to get over.

Next came my notification to the parish that I was leaving. I couldn't tell them that I was joining the Mormons. I wasn't sure at that time that I was going to take the big step. I told them that I loved them, and that if I were not leaving the pastorate I would rather serve them than be the pastor of any other church. I suspect many of them surmised we were looking toward the Mormons because I had been very open in expressing my admiration for The Church of Jesus Christ of Latter-day Saints.

There was a great burden on my heart. I had the feeling that I would never be well received by the Mormons because I had been a minister of another church. After all, I had not been born in the Mormon faith, and none of my ancestors had crossed the plains with covered wagons or handcarts.

I thought we might go to San Diego, California. There were many Mormon people in that city. The thought had come to me that I might earn a living as a professional fund-raiser and work for one of the large fund-raising organizations on the West Coast. I had some professional training in this field.

After our final Sunday in the Eggertsville Church in Buffalo, we had planned to make a brief visit to see our married daughter and her family in Indianapolis. We were there over a Sunday, and we attended an LDS ward. It was their fast Sunday; several high school young people bore their testimonies. My heart was deeply touched by these kids. I told my wife that I would give almost anything if I could feel as they did. She assured me that the time would come when I would have such a feeling.

We had one more project to complete before we could start west. We wanted to see the Book of Mormon Pageant at Palmyra. I told Bernice that we wouldn't dare go to Utah and admit to the Mormons that we had lived several years in Buffalo and had never attended the Book of Mormon Pageant. We returned to Palmyra one hot August day and witnessed the great pageant. That day when we came to the Hill Cumorah something happened to me. My burden rolled away, and my soul was flooded with joy as the missionaries gathered around us who had been guests in our home in Buffalo. I knew then that I wanted to be a member of The Church of Jesus Christ of Latter-day Saints more than I wanted anything in the world.

I was hardly aware of the great pageant; there was a greater drama going on in my heart after I had taken the big step and made the big decision. When we passed through Buffalo the next day to pick up our last mail delivery, there was a letter there from Ted and Florence Jacobsen inviting us to stay with them in Salt Lake City until we could get settled and knew what we wanted to do.

The trip to Salt Lake City was made with some difficulty. We had a serious automobile accident in Ohio that completely demolished our new car. But once in Salt Lake, it took only two or three days to complete arrangements for our baptism while we were living in the Jacobsen home.

About this time I made a careful written record of why I wanted to become a member of The Church of Jesus Christ of Latter-day Saints. There had been a volcanic eruption of emotion in my life as we confronted the change required of us in facing this new life. I was careful that my decision not be entirely motivated by emotion, but that it rest upon intellectual belief as well. I set down as carefully and as honestly as I could what my beliefs were concerning the Church. In the years since that time I have never felt the necessity of changing a single word of this statement of faith which I wrote shortly before I accepted baptism and became a member. This statement is as follows:

1.   After long and careful examination of the life and teachings of Joseph Smith, I am convinced that he is a prophet of God to the modern world as surely as Isaiah was to the ancient world. I believe that God the Father and his Son Jesus Christ did appear unto him and called him to be a prophet and revealed to him many great and precious truths. I believe his witness and teachings are true.

2.   I am convinced that The Church of Jesus Christ of Latter-day Saints is the true Church of Christ because I believe that its doctrines, articles of faith, and practices fit the scriptures of the Old and New Testaments more closely than the teachings of any other church.

3.   I believe that The Church of Jesus Christ of Latter-day Saints exalts Christ and gives him a place of preeminence he receives in no other Church.

4.   I believe that the Book of Mormon, the Doctrine and Covenants and the Pearl of Great Price are authentic, authoritative and are nearer the source of their origin than the Bible is to its origin, that they are inspired of God and divinely given and are therefore as binding upon us as the Bible. I believe these sacred writings contain the restored gospel of Jesus Christ to our modern world, that they contain the precious truths of our preexistence, the wonderful opportunities and privileges of our present existence and the glorious promises of our future life with God.

5.   I believe that the priesthood of The Church of Jesus Christ of Latter-day Saints is also authoritative and divinely given, that it was restored to the earth enabling the Church to be reestablished and to be guided by men who are called of God and given the authority to administer the ordinances of the gospel and to officiate in their several offices.

"Obey them that have the rule over you, and submit yourselves: for they watch for your souls, as they that must give account, that they may do it with joy, and not with grief . . . ." (Hebrews 13:17.)

6.   I believe in the continuous flow of the word of God through inspired prophets who have authority to receive prophecy. Such authority is not to be assumed, but is divinely given to him who has been called and ordained for this purpose, who continues to show himself worthy and is sustained by the voice of the Church.

7.   I believe the fruitfulness of The Church of Jesus Christ of Latter-

day Saints during the past century is a strong testimony to the truthfulness. Its accomplishments in colonization, education, industry, health, missionary service, and welfare are unique in world history, and its moral influence upon its youth is unequaled among all the churches of the world.

On the 17th day of August, 1959, we were all three baptized on Temple Square. On that same day there was an earthquake that did considerable damage in West Yellowstone National Park. There must be an underground subterranean connection between the Yellowstone Park and the tabernacle on Temple Square; a Congregational minister got baptized into the Mormon Church and the earth shook! It was indeed an earth-shaking experience for us.

I was baptized by Brother Truman Madsen. Bernice was baptized by Brother Ted Jacobsen and Fred by Henry Call, a missionary who had been close to him while we were in Buffalo. The wonderful experience of seeing my sweetheart come up out of the waters of baptism is something I shall never forget. Never had I loved her so much as I did then. I knew that we would be together forever in our Father's kingdom.

We were about ready to be on our way to California, but our life took a sudden turn in an unexpected direction. Bishop Joseph Wirthlin of the Bonneville Ward had recommended us for baptism. The people of that ward, especially Brother and Sister Jacobsen, felt some responsibility for our future. Elder Henry D. Moyle, who was in the First Presidency of the Church, suggested that I might serve in the Church School System as a seminary teacher. An interview was arranged with Brother William E. Berrett, Administrator of Seminaries and Institutes. Brother Berrett put me through a rough interview and was satisfied with my theological and academic qualifications as a prospective seminary teacher.

It was next arranged for Bernice and me to meet with one of the General Authorities of the Church for an interview. All prospective seminary teachers must be interviewed by a General Authority before they can be teachers in the system. Bernice and I met with Elder Hugh B. Brown. He has a large brass hourglass on his desk. When we were seated in his office he turned the glass over. He talked to us of the restoration of the gospel. He told us some things about the temple. We felt a warmth of love in the assurances he gave us that we had made a good choice in joining The Church of Jesus Christ of Latter-day Saints.

The sand had run through the glass, and we had continued with him long after the time of our appointment. The hour was late. He arose from his seat, and we quickly did the same, aware of the fact that we had overstayed our time. He came from around his desk, put one arm around my shoulder and the other around Bernice's shoulder, and drew us together and to himself in a firm embrace as he said these words.

"The Lord has prepared you to come to us."

I knew from that time on that we would be received and loved by the Mormons because we had all come from our Father's home, and we would be striving together to return again to our Father's home.

So I became a seminary teacher just ten days after my baptism! Every day that I am with the young people, I am aware of Elder Brown's words. The Lord has prepared me for this special, choice assignment where I continue to serve. When the new seminary was built at Skyline High School in Salt Lake City in 1962 I was assigned to be there, and I have continued there up to this time.

When I was confirmed by the laying on of hands, I was given the gift of the Holy Ghost, but apparently I was not spiritually ready or mature enough to receive this precious gift. A gift requires both a giver and a receiver. On Sunday, November 1, 1959, just two-and-a-half months after my baptism, the power of the Holy Ghost came down upon me. I stood in the sacrament meeting in our ward and gave my testimony. Quoting from Ephesians, second chapter, I stated my gratitude that we as a family were no longer "strangers and foreigners" to the gospel of Christ, but "fellowcitizens with the saints" in the Family of God. (Ephesians 2:19.)

As I stood in the chapel, the Holy Ghost came upon me and took my speech and my breath away. It was a joy beyond anything I had ever experienced. I didn't seem to need my breath for a short time. Had the Spirit remained with me very long, I am sure my body would have been shaken to pieces; it was a joy too great for the physical body to endure for long. This experience was to me the fulfillment of a promise the Lord had made to me some years before when I was pastor of the First Congregational Church at Riverhead, Long Island. There are personal aspects of this experience which I cannot put into speech or print, but it was a wonderful confirmation to me that we had indeed responded to the guidance of the Spirit by accepting the restored gospel.

The conversion story of an individual is never finished, because conversion is a continuing experience. I have a living hope which I share with my dear wife that we will see all of our children in the Church. We are grateful beyond any expression of words for the strong faith of our son, Fred, and for our sweet daughter and her wonderful husband who are active in the Church. Our son, Paul, and his dear wife, Barbara, are not members. We have a strong faith that they will be in the Church in time, because they are so good that they are not going to reject such an obviously good thing as the Church when they fully understand it and understand what it can do for them and their family.

On January 15, 1966, I was at prayer early in the morning, and the Lord came to me and gave me the Golden Sentence. He spoke the words to me as clearly as I ever heard them from a human tongue. My heart was overwhelmed with joy. I awakened Bernice and shared the Golden Sentence with her. We went to the BYU that day and I shared it with Fred. The joy this experience gave me in further confirming my testimony cannot be expressed.

Within the next few days something happened that brought me great distress. I used the Golden Sentence indiscriminately and too freely, and felt a severe condemnation of the Spirit. I was warned never to use the sentence unless I was directed by the Spirit to do so. Since that time I have used it only on a few occasions and always with a great spiritual effect.

I have been reluctant to put into print some of the experiences told in this story and have given the matter much deliberation. The decision to do so has been made with a good feeling and with the hope that members of my family and others who may read it will find it helpful and strengthening to their faith. I bear solemn witness to the reality of God and his love for us. I know that he is, and that he is the rewarder of them that diligently seek him. I know that Jesus Christ is God's Only Begotten Son in the flesh, and that it is only through his redeeming love that we may gain salvation by our repentance and our grateful acceptance of his atonement and our continuing obedience of all the laws of the gospel. I bear this witness in the name of Jesus Christ. Amen.

RUTH HUNSAKER

LIFE'S MAJOR GOALS REALIZED

*The Roman Catholic, Baptist, Christian Scientist, Methodist,
Presbyterian, and Unitarian Churches—Ruth Hunsaker examined
them all but they left her unsatisfied. So too did the more modern,
experimental groups of Christians.*

*Specifically, none of these organizations could answer the
two major questions that bothered her: (1) What about those who
have died without baptism? and, (2) Why does not the marriage
covenant extend beyond the grave? These questions were linked
with a strong feeling that she somewhere had a service to render.*

*Thus prepared mentally, she was perhaps a "natural" for the
gospel when it came to her. The interest of her account lies in the
way the doors were opened, sometimes miraculously, to the
fulfillment of her major goals in life when she found her two
main questions answered through the gospel. In those answers she
found true love and true service.*

For many years, I felt deep within my heart that somewhere
there was a service for me to render. Surely there was a work I
could do to justify my existence and to show my appreciation for
my many blessings. Since youth, my life was based on the first
two great commandments: the love of God and of fellowmen.
I was dedicated to demonstrating this love through service, but I
was puzzled as to what my purpose was in this life and where I
could best contribute service.

The second great need which I felt was religion. From age
eighteen, even though I had been raised in a home where there
was no formal religion practiced, I was dissatisfied and felt a

longing to know God. Although I investigated several churches, it was the Catholic religion which most intrigued me because of its claim of continuation since the Apostle Peter. I truly expected to find answers to life's major questions in Catholicism, but soon I became disenchanted. So three-and-a-half years later I left the Catholic Church, as I had not found the answers I had hoped for, and I could not accept many of the doctrines. Sincerely I wished to learn what is the true personality of God, so I began to read the Bible. Until then I had only studied Catechism.

Reading the Bible added two new problems to my list of unanswerables. I inherently believed, as many do, that a man and wife who have a true love for each other will be together forever. However, most Christian churches do not believe in eternal marriage; in fact, they have a marriage ceremony which states, "Until death do you part." I found the scriptural reason for this belief in the 22nd chapter of Matthew where it is stated; "For in the resurrection they neither marry nor are given in marriage, but are as the angels of God in heaven." This seemed an unhappy situation to anticipate.

The question which concerned me above all others was the Savior's statement to Nicodemus: "Verily, verily, I say unto thee, Except a man be born of water and of the Spirit, he cannot enter into the kingdom of God." (John 3:5). This caused me to worry about all the people who had come upon the face of the earth who would never be baptized. What about these unfortunate people? If God is a merciful and just God, would he unconditionally condemn them? No, surely he would provide a way for them. I made this a matter of prayer for many years not knowing why I was so concerned about the people who would never hear of the Lord Jesus Christ and never be baptized in their lifetimes.

Because of all these nagging questions, and a few lesser ones, I longed for guidance—and rationalized that I must become a part of an organization where I might cooperate with others who were seeking. I realized that everything the Lord has created is beautifully organized, and that I, too, must be in good order and serve and learn in an organized way. So I began to study various religious doctrines with a great desire to find a church that followed and defined the teachings of the Bible—one in which I could believe so completely that I would be happy to live all the principles.

I lived with a Baptist minister's family for almost a year; I attended the Christian Science church for two years; I studied Science of Mind, with Ernest Holmes, in Los Angeles; I studied and considered enrolling in the Unity School of Christianity at Lees Summit, Missouri. I attended the Methodist and the Presbyterian churches for a short time. I enrolled in a non-denominational group called "Camps Farthest Out." I believed, as they do, that the Spirit of the Lord is lacking in modern churches. They aspired to teach people about the power of prayer: how to pray effectively, the use of prayer circles for group prayers, and healing through prayer. I was also associated for a time with a group in Maryland called "Koinania," which teaches professional people to be missionaries overseas and at the same time practice their profession.

I was prayerful as I studied these religions and ideologies, but I never received an affirmative answer to my prayers that any of them was where I belonged. I never joined any of these groups.

Finally I came to Salt Lake City to take a graduate course in nursing at the University of Utah. For Christmas, a friend gave me the book, *A Marvelous Work and A Wonder*, by LeGrand Richards. I read the first four chapters quickly and felt for the first time that I understood the true personality of God the Father. I was deeply impressed by the explanation of the Apostasy, especially because of my background in the Catholic Church. I accepted that there had been a great falling away from the Church as Jesus Christ had established it while he was here on the earth.

The following Sunday was the first Sunday of the new year, and I decided to attend sacrament meeting in the ward where I lived. The guest speaker was a genealogist. I was so impressed by his talk that after the meeting I obeyed an urge and arranged for him to do my genealogical research.

As I continued to read, I discovered why I had been compelled to have my genealogical research begun. *I discovered why I had been so concerned about the people who go through life never hearing of Jesus Christ or being baptized.* For as our Savior and Redeemer gave his life on Calvary and vicariously took upon himself our sins, based upon our true repentance and obedience to his commandments, so that we may come back into his sublime presence, in a like manner we may give of ourselves and our time in genealogical research and attendance in a temple of the Lord— thus becoming saviors upon Mt. Zion receiving the essential ordinances such as baptism *vicariously* for those who have not had the privilege in this life. Paul wrote: "Else what shall they do which are baptized for the dead, if the dead rise not at all? Why are they then baptized for the dead?" (I Corinthians 15:29.)

It was obvious to me from this passage that baptism for the dead was also an ancient ordinance!

I was impressed also by the fact that The Church of Jesus Christ of Latter-day Saints was the only church I had investigated that teaches the principle of eternal marriage. It is the crowning ordinance of the gospel of Jesus Christ and is performed only in the temples of the Lord. The joining of a man and woman in holy matrimony for time and for all eternity *is* an earthly ordinance, and when performed by the authority of the Holy Priesthood, this union extends throughout eternity. I was grateful to find that eternal marriage is another ordinance which is performed vicariously for the dead. "Whatsoever ye shall bind on earth shall be bound in heaven." (Matthew 18:18.)

Within the next several weeks, I completed reading *A Marvelous Work and A Wonder.* In the process I had looked up all the scriptural references to be sure that they were quoted accurately and in context.

After fourteen years of searching, my many unanswered questions regarding religion had been satisfied. Everything seemed to fall into place; the whole plan of life and salvation came into view, with all the parts fitting as in a jig-saw puzzle. I had a sincere conviction, through the knowledge I had gained, that The Church of Jesus Christ of Latter-day Saints has the restored gospel of Jesus Christ.

And now for the next step: I pondered the author's challenge to follow the admonition of James, as did the Prophet Joseph Smith: "If any of you lack wisdom, let him ask of God, that giveth to all men liberally, and upbraideth not; and it shall be given him." (James 1:5.)

The author further stated, "You may never again, in this life, judge such an important matter. Your decision will follow you with its consequences through time and throughout the eternities to come."

I knelt in prayer, asking my Heavenly Father to manifest to me, through the power of the Holy Ghost, whether or not The Church of Jesus Christ of Latter-day Saints is the true Church. I made this a matter of prayer for several days; then I went to a sacrament meeting. As the sacrament was being passed, I was filled with the Spirit of the Lord, and my bosom burned within me. I knew the Lord had answered my prayers. I knew this was the restored gospel of Jesus Christ.

When I joined The Church of Jesus Christ of Latter-day Saints, my father disowned me, disinherited me, and never permitted me to come home again. My parents have now both passed away.

Since becoming a member of the Church, I have grieved for my parents who never had a knowledge of the gospel. I have grieved because we never knew what it was to have family prayer or to worship together, and because we never had the priesthood in our home.

I sensed a great responsibility resting upon me to do my genealogical research, as I am the only grandchild of my mother's or father's parents. My mother had seven brothers and sisters; I am the only child born of those eight children. My father is one of three children, and I am the only offspring of those three.

For the first thirteen years after joining the Church, I sought diligently, with the aid of five professional researchers, and was unable to add to my lines as much as one additional name. But through constant prayer and continued effort, with the aid of my sixth researcher, the floodgates of heaven have been opened. In the last year, I have been privileged to submit to the genealogical library, over eleven hundred family group sheets containing some five thousand names. I now have that many more names which I am preparing to submit. I had thought that if in my lifetime I could find two or three hundred names, I would be doing a great work. I am overwhelmed by the magnitude of this work when I think of over ten thousand people standing beyond the veil waiting for me to gather their names for them so that the ordinances essential for their eternal salvation may be performed.

Now that these records have come forth, and much of the ordinance work has been performed, the grieving I have felt for my family has almost been lifted from me, and a joy has filled my soul that is beyond my ability to describe.

I have been privileged to serve in the temples of the Lord for fourteen of the fifteen years I have been in the Church, including eight years as a set-apart temple worker. Serving in the temple has been the most soul-satisfying work I have ever done—the service for which I was searching. The veil is so thin between the living and those in the spirit world that you can almost feel their presence while performing the various ordinances. You are filled with an unusually sweet spirit that brings tears to your eyes and a swelling within your bosom as the Holy Ghost testifies of the efficacy of those sacred ordinances.

In addition to having a testimony of temple work, I have obtained a testimony of the principle of eternal marriage.

Some years before joining the Church I had a brief and disillusioning marriage. One child, a daughter, was born to this union. She also was of a religious nature, and she had intended to become a nun, but because of the influence of good friends she joined the "Mormon" Church at age fourteen—one year before I became a member. It was because of my darling child that I put myself through nurse's training, as I felt I must provide for her with a worthwhile occupation.

Six months after joining the Church I received my patriarchal blessing. Prior to my receiving that blessing, Patriarch Eldred Smith repeated three times the admonition:

"If you do not marry (in the temple) in this life do not be concerned. As long as you do not reject the new and everlasting covenant of eternal marriage, you will be given a worthy mate in the hereafter."

This was indelibly imprinted on my mind. I believed firmly in the doctrine of eternal marriage, and wondered how I could reject it. Throughout the years I discovered that there are several ways.

At the time I was living in California. I was sincere in associating only with men who were members of the Church. As the years went by, and I did not find a desirable companion, I thought that maybe I should try to convert an eligible nonmember although the Church authorities admonish the woman member not to become involved with a nonmember. They say, "Let the missionaries convert him, and let him prove himself."

I found that a nonmember, not having our same standards, often tends to draw one away from the high standards of the Church, even if this is not intentional. It occurs a little at a time and in small ways before one is aware what is happening. Fortunately I realized that this is the first step toward marrying outside of the Church and rejecting the new and everlasting covenant of eternal marriage!

Time continued to fly, and as I became older eligible men became more scarce. I could see the period of childbearing waning. In desperation I considered marrying a member of the Church who was lukewarm and not active. His habits had prevented him from honoring the priesthood, and he would not be able to take me to the temple. I suddenly realized again I was on the verge of rejecting the new and everlasting covenant of eternal marriage! The warning of the patriarch rang distinctly in my ears, giving me the courage to wait.

Fasting and prayer were essential to me, and I determined never to marry until the Spirit of the Lord testified to me that the man was the right one. Sometimes I fasted as many as three or four days for an answer. Throughout the years I never received an affirmative answer in this matter.

I knew that if I wanted the Lord to bless me, I must prove my worthiness and faithfulness by obeying the principles of the gospel, being active in the Church, accepting responsibility, and rendering service. This would be how I would meet a mate who was honoring the priesthood and would be eligible to marry in the temple.

One day in August the Spirit directed me: "You must go to Utah." I fasted three days over it, and the voice from within became louder and more distinct: "You must go to Utah."

"When! When?" I pleaded.

"Now!" Again loud and clear.

From a financial standpoint and because of the health of my aunt with whom I was living, I knew it would be better next year. But . . .

"Now!" the voice said.

I thought of a course I'd been interested in—Genealogy Technology—which was offered at the Brigham Young University. My, how I'd like to go to Provo and take that course! I prayed about it a couple of weeks.

I told my aunt. She had fallen and broken some ribs. ("How can I leave her?")

The Spirit directed, "You must go."

"I'll be back soon," I told my aunt.

"You'll never be back," she answered solemnly.

I went to Provo and attended the course on Genealogy. During the general conference that year, while I was working on memorizing some scripture, a voice again came to me and told me that I would marry a certain man and called him by name. It was President Hunsaker. But he was President of the Southern States Mission, and I was in Utah! I knew him because when we both resided in Los Angeles, I had attended his stake twice when there was a General Authority visiting. And sometime later in a Los Angeles newspaper I happened upon the notice of Sister Hunsaker's death. I sent a card of sympathy which President Hunsaker answered—a letter formally dictated to his secretary.

I was sure that he must be a very fine man, but we had never even held a conversation! How could I meet him again?

I finished one year of my course at the BYU and then had a very fine opportunity for an appointment as a nurse in Salt Lake City.

For a month I looked for an apartment in Salt Lake. I thought I would never find a suitable one, and when I did find one, it had already been rented just barely minutes before I was about to make the down payment. The man who was renting it stood with his back to me—but something told me, "if you ask that man, he will let you have that apartment!" Oh, no, I wouldn't do that, I thought, and left. I was very discouraged and bewildered as to why I had ever thought it was right for me to leave my excellent job in California and come to Utah. Nothing had turned out right.

It was not an easy year and I didn't see President Hunsaker (knowingly) until one year from the date the Spirit had told me that he was the man I would marry.

The worst possible thing happened when I finally saw him. I was attending a session of the temple in Salt Lake, when he came into the room. He approached, we shook hands, but he walked away as though he did not recognize me—in fact, he looked right through me! I was embarrassed because of all of my thoughts and the inspiration I had received about him. Yet I knew that none of it had been a dream. What I had heard, I had heard, and I knew that it was all true—somehow! But how would it ever come to pass? And how would I ever know if I could truly love him?

Then I saw him again in the temple four days after the encounter which had been such a disappointment. This time he stopped me and chatted with me, inquiring what I was doing in Utah.

The first time we were together after that was when he had invited me to go with him to the hospital to visit his sister who was ill. He gave her a blessing in my presence, and during that blessing I had a witness that I could love him and that he was the man I was to marry. On the way home, he told me he would like to show me where he lived, and took me to the very apartment house and pointed out the actual apartment which I had tried in vain to rent for myself! He had been the man who had rented that apartment, and he was still in the office with his back toward me the day I attempted to make a down payment.

I know without a doubt that the Holy Spirit directed all of these experiences, for he led me to the man who was to be my eternal mate and fulfill all of my aspirations and dreams—a man who has magnified his priesthood callings, served faithfully in the Church, and kept himself free from the pitfalls of the adversary. He is a former bishop, stake president, mission president, and counselor in the Salt Lake Temple Presidency. My cup runneth over with the bounteous blessings the Lord has poured out upon me, and I am thankful I had the faith to accept the counsel of the patriarch and wait for the right man.

The major goals of my life have been realized. After fourteen years of studying and searching, I found the true Church of Jesus Christ; after thirteen years of diligently seeking for my ancestors, thousands of names have come forth; and after twenty-five years of faithful waiting and loneliness, the Lord has given me an eternal companion.

MILO BAUGHMAN

THE AUTHENTIC CHURCH REVEALED

Milo Baughman is head of the Department of Environmental Design at Brigham Young University. How he got there is a story not only of innate talents and diligent application but also of great spiritual struggle.

Like many other converts, Milo Baughman lived for years only an arm's length away from the gospel, but could not perceive its truth. Before that period his life had led him from childhood belief on through youthful agnosticism then into the Presbyterian faith, where a great spiritual experience impelled him to a four-year study for the ministry. But remarriage, to an LDS girl, deepened the conflicts of life and accentuated his spiritual regressions.

Brother Baughman is a good example of the inadequacy of worldly success alone. Artistically talented, he moved from interior designing to free-lance furniture design and in this challenging environment made an enduring reputation as a distinguished pioneer designer of contemporary furniture. In the context of this high professional achievement with its rich material rewards his comment is revealing—without God "it all turned to dust in my mouth."

At 2:30 one morning Milo reached out his arm and the gospel was there waiting for him as it had been for years. The light broke upon his now-humble mind and heart as the skepticism of the past rolled away. The power of his testimony comes strongly through the following pages—the firm conviction of a man who tried the other routes and found them wanting.

My testimony, most simply stated, is that I would gladly give my life for this Church and for the special knowledge I have of Christ because of it. This is extraordinary, because I am not a brave man. In order to relate how this phenomenon came about, I must go back a few years.

I was not raised in any particular church, but was encouraged to go to Sunday School. My parents, now devout Lutherans, were not consistent churchgoers in those days. When I was about twelve, I fell into an argument with the minister of the church I then attended, regarding his unyieldingly literal concept of hell. Losing the argument, I abandoned church and became a thirteen-year-old agnostic. I had, and still have, warm memories of my intermittent experience in church before age twelve, especially visiting my grandfather's Methodist Sunday School class. I still remember very well the warm spirit among this group of old men. Actually, until my falling out I was probably more overtly religious than the average boy of my age.

Nevertheless, I became increasingly antagonistic to organized religion through my late teens and twenties. I had been raised in a moral, if not a pious way, and I felt strongly about ethics and personal morality. I concluded that this was sufficient and that only the weak and superstitious believed in and prayed to God.

At the end of my twenties and in my earliest thirties, following the breakup of an exceedingly unhappy marriage, I began to make an occasional stab at returning to church, but what I considered to be the mumbo-jumbo about the virgin birth, Christ's *physical* resurrection, and the other "miracles" sent me running again. Finally a very fortunate thing happened: *I became thoroughly miserable!*

Following my divorce I moved to New York City, set up my design office, and was soon making a great deal of money and a name for myself in my field. Materially and professionally I had everything I had ever dreamed of and which I had assumed, once obtained, would make me happy. But it all turned to dust in my mouth. I did not know then of Isaiah's admonition, "Wherefore do ye labor for that which satisfieth not?" (Isaiah 55:2.) Humbled by my abject unhappiness, I began in earnest to try church again. I had tried all the alternative possibilities, philosophical and otherwise. (I'll spare you the lurid details.) There was nothing left but the Christian alternative. In the meantime, I had the examples of my sister and parents who had all become very serious in and much benefited by their Lutheran faith.

This time it clicked. I had found in a nearby Presbyterian Church a very literate and powerful preacher, as well as a very attractive group of people my age. Their warm acceptance was crucial to my reapproach to the Christian faith.

But after a series of good experiences, I began to regress again. One must struggle—pay the price—to be a good Presbyterian, just as he must to be a good Latter-day Saint. I found myself once more quite despondent. But thanks to sermons I had heard recently, somewhere in my memory was the message concerning repentance. Luther said that "the Holy Ghost can only come to a broken and contrite heart." This described my condition perfectly. For the first time I was truly contrite. My whole life seemed a foolish sham. For the first time I knelt in prayer. For the first time I spoke the words out loud. And for the first time I truly repented of my sins—a whole lifetime of excesses, pride and foolishness. For the first time I unreservedly confessed my complete inadequacy without God; I recognized with great clarity that I simply could not make it without his help.

This produced a moment I shall never forget. I sensed the actual presence of Christ in that room that night. I felt as if he actually stood beside me and gently placed his hand on my shoulder. And with this touch, I felt forgiven. There had been much, very much, in my past to be forgiven. The flood of relief and joy that came to me in that hour is impossible to describe.

My discovery of this new and infinitely more meaningful dimension in life—in short, the experience of being forgiven and of starting fresh—was quite overwhelming. Nothing else held my interest now, including my design career. I felt impelled to study for the ministry. I was accepted at Bangor Theological Seminary in Maine. I closed up my office and went to California to visit my parents for the summer while I awaited the start of classes in the fall.

I prayed that I would be guided in all things that summer—for example, as to whether or not I should marry again and when. I didn't expect the answer so soon. But one afternoon I felt as if I were being picked up by the scruff of my neck and propelled by the Lord to Carolyn's door. (Carolyn and I had been engaged twelve years earlier, but the war changed our plans. We each married different people. She, too, was now divorced. I had seen her two summers previously, but her rediscovery of her Mormon faith which she had pretty much abandoned when she married outside the Church had discouraged my further interest. Now, her "religiousness" was in her favor.) I found myself in front of her door, reappearing without ceremony after a two-year absence, asking her to marry me. Apparently propelled by the same spirit as I was, she said yes.

We had a bad moment or two when we later considered the possible problems of a Mormon girl being married to a Presbyterian minister, but with the advice of a respected counselor we got over that hurdle and proceeded. I was exceedingly happy to have Carolyn and my two new children, Gary (ten) and Deb (four) with me!

Our four years at Bangor Theological Seminary were very difficult. As it became apparent to both of us that the differences between our faiths were much greater than we had imagined, and it became clear that Carolyn could not join with me as a pastor's wife in the work of a typical parish minister, I decided that ordination was impossible. I felt terrible conflict, as did Carolyn, over this decision. I had four very hard years invested in my education and training as a minister, and I could still not shake the feeling that I had been "called" to a special service in the church.

But there's more to it than that. In some ways I had lost my faith, or at least much of the enthusiastic certainty I had had when I first arrived at Bangor Seminary. To qualify this a bit, I should say that I had not lost my faith in God, so much as in the church. (In time, of course, this kind of doubt will affect our faith in God and Christ, for we ask ourselves, If Christ is Christ and the head of this church, why is its history so full of failure, and why is it so ineffectual in its present state?) All this led to a serious emotional breakdown. Several years of extreme depression and regular psychotherapy followed.

My declining confidence in the part of the Christian church I was involved in, and my struggle to regain my emotional health, were not helped much by the service I tried to give for five years as a better-trained layman in a suburban Presbyterian church. I was often inspired by the minister and by different individuals in this church, and in the Christian church at large, but I grew increasingly discouraged with the church itself. I tried to help several lost friends, including one who was alcoholic, by bringing them to church. It didn't work, and it was no longer working for me. The spirit was gone. This is when I knew I must find something stronger, something more authentic, and find it fast.

My search ultimately led me to a period of total despair, and for the first time since my encounter with Christ and the experience of being forgiven nine years earlier, I did not go to church at all for a few Sundays. It is impossible to describe to one who has not experienced it the sense of grief that comes with the realization that the church one has loved is not the right one. I began to search again. I came upon a small group of equally disheartened Christians who had broken away from the established Protestant church to form a "fellowship of seekers." (I discovered that there were many such groups in the United States.) But the new zeal I felt in this group was spoiled by Carolyn's stubborn refusal to acknowledge that it was the real thing, the *authentic* church I had been searching for. This "wet blanket" response led to a very serious showdown between Carolyn and me. Our religious ruptures had never been this threatening before.

The tension built day after day. With a very troubled heart one evening, I said my second major prayer for repentance. It hurt, but I admitted that maybe I didn't have all the answers, that my "orthodox" view of the Christian faith might not be entirely right after all, in spite of all my theological learning. For the first time I asked with an open mind and heart to know whether the Mormon Church was true. (Always before, keeping my routine promise to Carolyn, I had said in an occasional prayer, "Dear Lord, if the Mormon Church is true, please let me know—but of course I know it isn't.")

I was awakened at 2:30 a.m. Something told me to get up, go downstairs, and open the Bible. I did not hear a voice giving me exact instructions, yet the thought was unmistakably clear and compelling. I could not help but obey this impulse. I went straight to my reading chair, picked up the Bible and turned immediately to James. This was odd, for this was a book in the New Testament I had never liked. In fact, my only A-plus paper while at Bangor Seminary was a highly critical treatment of this "Epistle of Straw." (So labeled by Luther.)

My eyes first fell on verse 24 of chapter 2: ". . . by works a man is justified, and not by faith only." This was precisely what Luther (and I) plus all other doctrinal Protestants did not like about James. This emphasis on works seemed so totally contradictory to Luther's emphasis on salvation coming strictly from faith, or "grace alone."

Then another scripture seemed to jump from the page (verse 10 of chapter 2): "For whosoever shall keep the whole law, and yet offend in one point, he is guilty of all." These two scriptures suddenly made sense! Along with most enlightened Protestants, I had previously been much disturbed by what appeared to be the Mormon emphasis on *"earning"* salvation and on what I termed an excessive legalistic stress on special disciplines like the Word of Wisdom, etc. Now, out of the blue, both the scriptures (and all that surrounds them in James) had become beautifully clear and profoundly meaningful! It was a remarkable feeling. I know what true enlightenment feels like.

Then the thought came to me, Who has been teaching these things all along? Joseph Smith, that's who! The very man who I had earlier concluded was probably an ingenious fraud. I closed the Bible and picked up from near my chair a book which was a compilation of the teachings of Joseph Smith. (I had intended to read this book to build my case against this "so-called prophet.") I read with increasing excitement. Everything in this book was extraordinarily clear, and seemed more correct, more authentic, than anything I had ever read. A feeling of warmth and indescribable happiness and calm came over me, beyond anything I had ever experienced before. I knew without any doubt whatsoever that Joseph Smith was literally, absolutely, unequivocally a true prophet of God. This fact in turn validated the authority of The Church of Jesus Christ of Latter-day Saints, the Book of Mormon, and all subsequent teachings of the leaders of this Church!

This was an exhilarating moment. When an aggressive disbeliever falls, he falls hard.

I realized with a joyous rush at about 5 a.m. that I wanted to be baptized more than anything else in the world. But almost at once grievous doubts of the consequences swept over me. What would my Lutheran family say? What about the Mormon Church's position regarding the Negro that troubled me so? There were other sudden doubts. These concerns almost did me in.

I prayed to know what to do, and the answer was unmistakable: You have enough testimony. Suspend judgment on these issues for a while. Understanding will come. (And it has, but that's another story.) Go and wake up Carolyn and the kids and tell them you are going to be baptized as soon as it can be arranged.

So I did. It was a great moment. Carolyn, of course, refused to believe it. After nine hard years, who would believe it?

Skeptical Mormon friends turned out in droves to witness my baptism, presumably because they wouldn't be convinced unless they could see it with their own eyes. I went around for several days in such a state of happiness that I concluded that either (1) I had died and gone to heaven, or (2) the whole thing was only a dream. Fortunately, I was wrong on both counts.

There have been many ups and downs since. The first year is especially rough for most converts, and perhaps was more so in my case. I had so much unlearning to do. My total unreserved acceptance of the Book of Mormon came slowly, as did the conviction that the Church was led by a living prophet. But when I gained a testimony of these things, and much, much more, my new-found convictions made the preceding struggle well worthwhile.

My stand as a member of The Church of Jesus Christ of Latter-day Saints has become very firm, and for this I humbly thank my Father in heaven every day of my life. I pray that I will never take this great gift for granted; I intend to pray always that I will "endure to the end." The anchor a testimony provides has gotten me through several severe recurrences of the depression that followed my breakdown. It will get me through anything that might come. And it will help get my dear wife and children through anything as well.

To have a testimony that this is literally the true Church, that it was established by our Savior, that it is still led by him through a living prophet and apostles, that it will someday redeem the whole world, and that in some way I am a part of all this, is to be given a sense of purpose and an excitement about life that makes all the difference. I wish I could put it much more dramatically. To have to put such a giant feeling into such puny words is very frustrating.

All this explains, in part, what I meant earlier when I said I would gladly die rather than deny my testimony of Christ and his church—in spite of my not being a brave man. I hope with all my heart that my sharing these things will be of worth to someone.

MANGAL DAN DIPTY

CONVERSION IN KASHMIR

At the conversion of Cornelius, the Apostle Peter expounded an important concept: ". . . in every nation he that feareth [God], and worketh righteousness, is accepted with him." (Acts 10:35.) The statement is as apt for the sole member from India in the twentieth-century Church as it was for the lone Roman soldier in the apostolic Church.

The son of devout Christian parents, Mangal Dan Dipty was a youthful Pentecostal minister when he first read of the Church while in Kashmir, India. An unusual feature of his story is that the Spirit gave him the initial witness on the basis of an anti-Mormon article. Thereafter Mangal had to maintain his faith and testimony for years, with absolutely no other Church associations in the vast country of India and with only his prayers and the slender lifeline of correspondence with the Church in Salt Lake City to sustain him spiritually.

Through special arrangement, Brother Dipty was baptized in 1961 in a muddy river in India. By persistent faith and works he somehow managed to get to Canada seven years later and thence to the United States. Here at Brigham Young University he was able to realize the two great desires of his heart—to associate with the saints and to learn the gospel of Jesus Christ so that he can serve the Lord better in his native land.

"I am glad to write to you that I am baptized . . . by Apostle Kimball on 7th January, 1961, in the river Yammuna at New Delhi. . . . Now I have given up my job and left the building, property, etc. of the (Pentecostal) Church . . . . Please remember me in your prayers that I can stand for the truth and can be used for the good of others." Thus wrote Mangal Dan Dipty—the first of India's 600,000,000 (according to Church records) to be baptized on native soil in 106 years—in a letter dated January 12, 1961, five days after the event took place.

Brother Dipty's grandfather had served as a priest in the Hindu temples. In the 1890's, German missionaries converted him to the Lutheran faith. When he became a Christian, his ancestral name was changed from Prahraj to Dipty. His grandson, Mangal Dan, was the third of five children and was born in Murtahandi, which is situated at an elevation of 5,000 feet above sea level in the rolling foothills of the Himalaya Mountains.

The home of the Dipty family was a very comfortable one surrounded by orchards and garden. Mr. Dipty ran a clothing and tailoring business and employed several servants, both in the shop and in the home. Hunger and want were strangers to this household of plenty. Mrs. Dipty named her third son Mangal, meaning "good," and, being a very loving and spiritual lady, she taught her children the stories of the Bible and how to pray.

At the early age of eight, Mangal Dan developed a great admiration for his Lutheran ministers and missionaries, and a great love for the Lord. One of the highlights of his childhood was to be allowed to stand on the pulpit and announce the hymns in behalf of his favorite German missionary. The experience grew into a strong desire to dedicate his life to serving the Lord when he grew older. In his late teens, Mangal Dan studied for three years in a theological seminary in India, which prepared him at the age of 21 to assume the assistant pastorship of a Pentecostal congregation. The Pentecostal Church appealed to him both spiritually and morally. It was a strict sect of modestly dressed members who were admonished not to smoke, drink, or attend movies.

During his first vacation, the apprentice pastor journeyed to a mountain tourist resort in Kashmir. There he borrowed a book from the local library to while away his time. The book told of the heresies which had crept into Christianity, and here Mangal discovered the existence of The Church of Jesus Christ of Latter-day Saints. The introduction given to his new discovery was so unfavorably phrased that it caused him to wonder in his heart at the unreasonable accusations made by the writer in the article entitled, "Is Mormonism Christianity?"

While he pondered and wondered, his mind was illuminated and he received certain knowledge that the Church he was reading about was the true Church and that it taught the true doctrine. Astounded at the experience, and not knowing what to do next, Mangal Dan prayed that he might know where to find this Church. A day or two later, his eyes fell upon a footnote connected with the same article which indicated that the headquarters of the Mormon Church was in America in Salt Lake City, Utah. Using this for an address, he dropped a card in the mail and waited and hoped.

His card found its way to the desk of LaMar S. Williams in the Missionary Department and initiated a correspondence between the two which was to prove Mangal's "lifeline" to the Church for the next eight years. Brother Williams sent him the Book of Mormon and other books and pamphlets and bore his testimony by letter. In August of 1960, Mangal Dan wrote: "I am very much thankful to God and to you for your books. I have read them often and have fully understood by the help of the Holy Spirit. I believe the Book of Mormon is really the word of God and would like to join in your Church to do the Lord's work as his will."

At the end of 1960 Elder Spencer W. Kimball of the Council of the Twelve was on an extended tour of the furthermost areas of the Church. Brother Williams managed to contact him in New Zealand, and Elder Kimball was able to reschedule his plans and arrange to meet with Brother Dipty for three days in New Delhi, two hundred miles south of his home in Dehradun. Elder Kimball told Brother Dipty that his congregation would leave him if he were baptized, and he would have very difficult times to face. Brother Kimball suggested that it might be better not to baptize Brother Dipty at that time and leave him there all alone without Church affiliation. Mangal Dan's reply was, "I will do what you want me to do, but I will go back disappointed, because I have traveled far to be baptized."

On the third day of his visit, January 7, 1961, Elder Kimball granted Brother Dipty the desire of his heart and baptized him. Elder Kimball had no baptismal clothes in his luggage, so he wore his second best suit for the ordinance. Together the two men waded into the River Yammuna. The river consisted mainly of mud, and when the water reached their waists, the mud came to their knees. The people on the bank began to look on in interest and curiosity at the sight of an American wading in his suit. Finally the two men came to a place where the water was deep enough, and Brother Dipty was baptized. Upon reaching the bank, Elder Kimball noticed that he had failed to remove his travel papers from his pockets; they had to be laid on newspapers to dry before he returned to the hotel, where he confirmed Brother Dipty a member of the Church.

Brother Dipty had assured Elder Kimball that his congregation would support him in everything he did, but as his letter of January 12, 1961 indicated, he was on his own only five days later. "You have gone astray," they accused him. "You are ill and have had hallucinations!" But Brother Dipty bore his testimony fervently to his congregation. He assured them he was not insane, that he actually had heard a voice bearing record that he had indeed discovered God's true Church.

In a letter dated May 20, 1961, he wrote, "I still have not got any job . . . . Do you know that my father and my relations asked me to go home and return unto Pentecostal faith and live happy life, but I utterly refused because I know this is the only true Church in the world established by God himself."

On June 1, he continued, "Brother, I think it a sin to keep tithing with me. I am in a hurry to hand it over to any bishop. I started to keep tithing from my baptism. I put all this money in a separate bag. Still I am unemployed, but I get wages in some time when I work odd jobs, e.g., coolie in city and in villages . . . . I have three one dollar bills with me, so I want to offer these little coins for the Church welfare work . . . I am very much thankful to God for his abundant grace. I came out from darkness to the light. Now I am in the right path and have to walk far more. So I earnestly request you to teach and guide me according to the word of God for the benefit of my life. Remember me in your prayer."

Even prior to his baptism, Mangal Dan had written: "Whenever I get the chance to speak, I tell about the testimony of Joseph Smith the Prophet of God. It is absolutely new for many. No one ever heard of this glorious message in this place." In the course of events, he later secured a little two-room apartment. In one of the rooms he started an LDS Gospel Center. He would distribute literature and get ten, fifteen, or more people interested, but he could not hold their interest because he ran out of answers to their progressive questions. Brother Dipty thus came to the realization that he was terribly handicapped in India and needed to go where he could become more fully acquainted with the organization and teachings of the Church.

During these years, a compassionate soul who loved the Lord and his fellowmen made it possible for Mangal Dan Dipty to attend Aggra University, where he obtained his B.A. degree in 1967, majoring in psychology. His desire and determination to live the gospel and to one day be with the saints hurdled him over many barriers. With encouragement from nobody, he silently cut the "red tape" and arrived in Canada in September of 1968 with only eight dollars in his pocket. He worked in Coutts, Alberta, until he could obtain a ten-day visitor permit for the United States and make the last stage of his long-dreamed-of journey. On May 21, 1969, he walked unannounced into the office of Brother LaMar S. Williams.

Armed with nothing but faith and determination to stay in the U.S., he saw his ten brief days begin to pass. While receiving a haircut, Brother Dipty engaged in conversation with the barber, Brother Arthur Sommerfeld, who is a convert from Germany. They talked about how each of them had joined the Church. Several other customers listened with interest. When the haircut was completed, a man rose and offered to pay for the service. This stranger later contacted Brother Dipty at his hotel room and invited him for dinner the following day. During the dinner conversation, he offered to give Mangal Dan Dipty $1,000 to provide for one year of education at the Brigham Young University in Provo, Utah.

Brother Dipty had previously visited the BYU campus but had dismissed the possibility of ever attending that University because of the high expenses involved. This unexpected opportunity enabled him to secure a student visa.

This turn of events not only permitted him to remain in Utah and go to school there, but also to fulfil his dream of fellowshipping with the saints and of increasing his knowledge and understanding of the restored gospel. One of the happiest days of Mangal Dan Dipty's life was September 20, 1970, when he was ordained an elder of the Church and received the Melchizedek Priesthood.

After emerging from eight years of a "Robinson Crusoe" type of existence (to put it in his words) as a lone Mormon among India's millions, Mangal Dan Dipty has accepted his brief exposure to the programs of the Church with the simple faith without which nobody can please his Maker, yet with a desire to adjust and become part of all that is expected of him. When things look impossible to him, he will remember the trials and blessings of the past and, confidently facing the future, will say, "The Lord will provide."

This account was written by Erika Dodds, a convert from England employed in the Church Missionary Department.

HELMA HAHN

A PROMISE KEPT IN ROTTENBURG

Like the proverbial bumblebee, the young missionary did not know that it couldn't be done. Impressed by the picture of the famous old house in the ancient German city, he determined that he would be the means of converting someone who lived there. He carried this resolution throughout his mission.

Elderly Helma Hahn lived alone in the house. The missionary's inspiration was vindicated when she proved receptive to the gospel. Looked down on by the other citizens, she thanks God for the gospel, for the missionaries who brought it to her, and for the LDS visitors from far and wide who are constantly calling on the "only Mormon in town."

———————

The background for the conversion of Sister Hahn of Rottenburg (pronounced Rō-ten-bearg), Germany, goes back to the Language Training Mission (LTM) in Provo, Utah. The cover of the textbook used by the missionaries to study German, called *Deutsch fur Missionare*, features a picture of one of the most famous houses in the medieval city of Rottenburg. While studying in the LTM, an Elder Stobbe, knowing only that he was called to go to the Germany South Mission and not realizing that Rottenburg was not open to missionaries, became enchanted with the romance this picture represented. As he studied, he made a silent vow to himself that he would bring the gospel to someone in that house. He did not then know that only one person lives in this famous old house—Helma Hahn.

Near the end of his mission Elder Stobbe was transferred to Ansbach, about twenty miles from Rottenburg. Knowing this was as close to Rottenburg as he would get, he went with his companion to Rottenburg to search out the house pictured on the textbook. It was easy to find, because it is one of the most photographed houses in Rottenburg, which in turn is the most photographed city in Germany.

The door on the ground floor was open, so the elders entered, walked up the steep, ladder-like stairs and knocked on the door of elderly Helma Hahn's living room. The two elders were each about six feet tall. The little house is more than five hundred years old, and the ceilings are quite low.

Sister Hahn relates her experience in these words: "I answered the knock at the door and was immediately shocked and frightened to find two giants standing before me. I would have closed the door but for their smiling, pleasant faces and honest look. They introduced themselves as missionaries of The Church of Jesus Christ of Latter-day Saints. When I heard the name of Jesus Christ and Latter-day Saints I was impressed, and I thought to myself, 'They cannot be bad men.'

"I invited them to come in. They told me the story of the restoration of the gospel. After they had finished their discussion, they asked if they might hold a prayer with me. Because of this, I invited them to return.

"As they continued to teach me, my feelings of having been brought the truth increased rapidly. I knew it would be necessary for me to be baptized again because my earlier baptism as a child was invalid, but I was fearful. My legs are not good, and it is difficult for me to get around, so I wondered how the baptism could be performed. However, I was determined to do it—and with the Lord's help I did! I made my own baptismal dress especially for this event, and upon it I used the embroidery I had been keeping for my burial dress."

Most of Sister Hahn's neighbors are members of the same families who have lived in Rottenburg for centuries. They dislike and are suspicious of change—and have kept their little city very much as it was in the twelfth century. They turn their backs on Helma Hahn since she has become Rottenburg's sole Mormon, this being the attitude she predicted but hoped would not occur. She is consoled in the knowledge that she has done the right thing, and she loves the restored gospel with all her heart. She enjoys sitting at her table by the window and reading the Book of Mormon which is always open there. Now she receives many letters and more visitors than she ever had before in her life—new friends from all over the world, so many Latter-day Saint tourists come to Rottenburg and the news gets around that she is there alone.

What is most important, there are many, many things to learn and very little time to do it in, as the gospel reached her very late in her life. She is very grateful to the special missionary who knew in his heart that there was someone there in Rottenburg who was ready to hear the message—someone who wouldn't mind being "the only Mormon in town."

> *Information about the conversion of Sister Hahn was supplied by Orville Gunther, former President of the Germany South Mission.*

EMIL POOLEY

A HOPI PROPHECY FULFILLED

When Emil Pooley's old uncle told him not to accept initiation into his native Hopi Indian religion, his words were prophetic —"You will know when the right religion comes to you."

The prophecy took several years to reach fulfillment. When LDS missionaries found Emil and his wife, the couple recognized some amazing similarities between the new message and their old Hopi beliefs—similarities which will intrigue the reader of the account which follows. Accepting the persecution it would involve, the family joined the Church.

Emil Pooley and his wife live with their family in Arizona. Strong in the faith, they look forward to serving a mission to the Hopi people when their younger children are raised.

It was past time to be initiated an elder in our Hopi Indian religion, but I'd been away working for the Sante Fe Railroad, so as a candidate for initiation I was "over-ripe." I did not belong to any church. When I arrived where my mother lives, my old uncle was waiting for me. He was an ancient man. He looked at me with his watery eye, and asked, "Is that you?"

I said, "Ya."

"Good," he said. "I hope I'm in time. I heard they are going to initiate the young men into the religion to become elders. Has your godfather asked you yet? Has he talked to you about it?"

I said, "No."

He said, "Good. I'm in time. All right. You listen to me real closely, what I'm going to tell you. You do it. You are *not* to join this Hopi religion. You are to join some other belief, some other religion—what religion, I don't know. But you are to join that, and you are to study that religion, and when you have learned, you are to come to our people and teach them."

He said further, "You will know when the right religion comes to you; you will know it. This is all I have to say. But I forbid you to join the Hopi religion, so don't do it! I have been waiting for you here for a long time to tell you this."

My uncle went home. Years passed. The time came when I was living in Winslow, Arizona, a married man with three children. The Latter-day Saint missionaries were laboring there with little success. Everybody slammed the door in their faces and would have nothing to do with the Mormons. While I was at work, my wife let the two elders come in. That night they came back because she had made an appointment with them to see me. I didn't want to have anything to do with them, but my wife insisted I listen, and later on I began to ask questions. For two or three weeks they taught us the gospel. Two lady missionaries came also. The ladies were discouraged because they couldn't get into any house. They could come to us, and we were good to them.

I didn't join the Church just like that, quickly. I studied it, and I thought about my people—what they stand for, what I had been taught ever since I could remember. I looked at my people and remembered my old uncle's words, how their religion was dying off—how he said the Hopi religion was man-made. So I thought about it—about it coming to an end pretty fast—and I thought about my children. I compared our religion to that of the Latter-day Saints and what I had learned in that short time. I believed that the LDS faith was the true religion that my old uncle had told me would be taught to me.

I reasoned: If I join the Mormon Church I will raise my family in that line. I will teach them, and they will be taught these things. They will live this better way. But we will be persecuted, and our friends will make fun of us.

I thought about this quite a lot, and finally I made the decision. It was a pretty hard thing to do. I did not like to give up our old way of life. I closed my eyes, held my breath, and reached for Mormonism, saying, "I'll take it!" I felt deeply that the things the missionaries taught were true.

One evening while we were eating, I asked the elders, "Elders, when can we be baptized?"

They looked at one another and said, "Saturday."

That was on Thursday. So they made the arrangements at Joseph City, twenty miles east of where we were, and we were baptized.

Sure enough, I was persecuted. My wife used to cry because of it, and I felt sorry for her. But Brother and Sister Anderson from Springville were there at that time, so they helped us along. For instance, instead of riding a car to the church, Brother Anderson and I would get our Books of Mormon and our Bibles under our arms, and we would walk to our church, in front of all my friends. I wasn't very strong then, but this kind of experience gave me a little courage. After a month or so I was ordained a deacon, and within a year, an elder. My wife and I went through the Mesa Temple and also had our children sealed to us.

I'd like to tell you about one experience I had. In Mesa we stayed with a Sister Black. She's a widow who had extra room in her home, so she gave us a room with two double beds in it. I had a dream that night in which we were staying in that very house, and I was in the kitchen, sitting reading the Book of Mormon, Someone came in the front door. I looked up, and it was my father who had died some few years before.

I said, "Father, what are you doing here?"

He said, "Son, I'm glad to see you. I have come to bring you a message. You are going to the temple tomorrow. I am very happy for you and your family. It is the right thing to do." (His endowment had been done previously.) And then he continued:

"When you get back home, you tell your mother to join our Church, because I know for myself now that it is true. I long for her, and I want her to be with me when it is time for her to come.

So you do that for her." In my dream he left me, and I closed the Book of Mormon.

I have had a lot of such experiences—many different things.

My wife and I have raised all of our seven children, and now four of them have been married in the temple.

I know that the gospel is true. There are a great many things about it that correlate with the Hopi beliefs. For one thing, the Hopis were told that they should accept the religion that would be brought to them by their true white brothers.

We believe that when our ancestors first came here, the white men came with them. The Indians didn't come by themselves. White people and dark people came together. And we did not come from the north country as some white men believe, because the Hopis say the country is too cold up there. We couldn't have come that way, and there are no ruins up that way. But we did come from the south; we migrated up this way.

Our belief also is that the white man, after we had separated, went eastward. How far they went after they left our people, we don't know. We didn't keep track of them. But the Hopis have two sets of records which they received by the Spirit. These are duplicates—there are another two sets. One of these sets was given to the white man, and its duplicate to the Hopis. Then one of the other sets was given to the same white men, and the duplicate of that was given to another Hopi. Those things are still in existence out in Hopi villages. When "they" come, they are to bring records, and these records will compare with our Hopi records. If they are both the same, those bringing them are true white brothers that we've been waiting for.

I think we are waiting for the LDS people to come. I believe this because the Mormon's religion is very much like that of the Hopi. For instance, at one place in their ceremony the Hopis baptize for the dead. Another similarity is that the Hopis believe that this earth will become celestialized, and that the good people will inherit the earth, and that there will be three places for mortals to go.

When I was just a boy my other old uncle used to tell the children in our family about that time which is to come. He said that if we are living in sin rather than in the right way, our white brother will come in anger. He will whip us. It will be so terrible a time that a lot of people's hearts will fail them, and they will die. And a lot of people will try to hide themselves under rocks and different things, and they won't be able to hide themselves. But the good people will have a good feeling in their hearts. Then, my uncle told us, our white brother will separate us, and all these bad people will quickly be taken to another place, just in the time it takes to blink an eye. And there they will cry because the place will be dark. Pretty soon they will see the light coming from the east, and they will say, "Look, there's the sun coming up." So they will stop crying and look, but when the light comes up, it will be a moon. And it will go down, and all will be dark again, and again they will cry. Then they will see another light coming up, and they will say again, "Look, here it comes. Surely it is the sun this time." But it will be a moon again. There will be no sun. Those people will be living in a world which is lighted only by a moon.

As for the most wicked people—the killers, those who are practicing witchcraft and things like that—they will go farther underneath where there will be no light. There everyone will be weeping all the time.

In telling us children about these three places, my uncle would tell us to shut our eyes very tight, and then he'd ask: "Can you see?"

"No," we would reply.

"Well, that's the way it will be in the dark places. So you be good, and be ready when your white brother comes. We older folks thought it was going to be in our time, but I see it probably won't be, but it may be in your time. If it isn't in your time, then it will be in your children's time, or in your children's children's time. But it will come."

There are many Hopi beliefs that are close to LDS beliefs. I will mention one more in particular, which in the Church we call the Word of Wisdom. My grandmother used to tell us children not to drink anything hot. She told us not to drink coffee because it was too strong for us. And the old folks used to tell us: "Don't smoke. It's not good for you. It will soften up your body and harm your blood, and make you get old quickly. Just let us old people smoke, because we don't inhale the smoke; we pray with it."

When I go to the Hopi reservation, I talk with people about the LDS Church. Some of them seem interested, though they do not join. One of them told me: "I cannot join your church. I know it's true; I believe what it teaches, but I can't join it."

I asked him to explain why.

"I'll tell you," he said, "When we joined the Hopi religion, we made an oath that we would never depart from this religion, from this belief, and that we would always stick to it."

"What would happen to you if you departed from it?"

"Well, our lives would be taken. If we were to depart from this religion when we have promised we would not—do you know what would happen?" he asked.

"No," I replied.

He then made a motion of slitting his throat.

When my wife and I finish raising our last three children, we want to go on a mission to the Hopi people and preach the gospel to them in their native tongue. This will enable us to bring to them the truth which has meant so much to us. It will fulfill the request and the prophecy which my old uncle made years ago.

JUAN SORIANO

THE SHINING WORDS

*In these days when "old men shall dream dreams, [and] . . .
young men shall see visions," some conversion experiences are
bound to come in such form. Juan Soriano's did.*

*Of Lamanite ancestry, Juan had barely reached his middle
teens at the time of his conversion and was living in the pueblo
of Chalco, Mexico, where he was born and reared. His pueblo was
one of the first to hear the gospel message in the heart of Mexico.
Courageously Juan forsook the Catholic faith and the related
teachings of his parents and embraced the gospel.*

*Great blessings have resulted for Juan and his family, who
are among the most dedicated Church members in Mexico. Several
of the children have served or are serving full-time missions, and
some of the older ones hold college degrees. Through such experiences the family members have greatly broadened their horizons,
at the same time insuring for themselves and their posterity the
more abundant life foreshadowed by the shining words Juan saw
on a night forty years ago.*

Juan Soriano was born and reared in the pueblo of Chalco,
Mexico. Flowing in his veins is the blood of his Lamanite
ancestors. He has the appearance of one of the Aztec race. He
was born into humble circumstances, but has a great heritage.

Juan's pueblo was one of the first where the gospel was
carried to the people in the heart of Mexico. Indeed, that area
could well be called the cradle of Mormonism in the Mexican
Mission. Juan was only a boy then. "It was the year of 1932," he

recalls, "when I first heard the message of the Mormon mission-aries. It happened on an occasion when one of my school friends invited me to be a guest in his home. As we sat around the table to eat, I was surprised to feel a spirit of reverence as they blessed the food and gave thanks to the Lord for his gracious love and protection. I was greatly impressed that the simple prayer was terminated in the name of Jesus Christ.

"After the meal, I was introduced to two young elders—two missionaries. Soon we were engaged in a religious discussion. I sensed a feeling of happiness during this conversation, and was astounded at the knowledge of the young missionaries. I was fifteen years of age at that time. Having been taught by Catholic priests since an early age, these words of the Gospel of Saint Matthew came to my mind: 'And the day will come when they will raise up false prophets, and many will be deceived.'

"I asked myself, 'Could the Savior have been referring to these young elders?' Then doubts began to enter my mind; ques-tions began to bother me, and I felt that I could not think clearly."

One of the missionaries gave Juan a copy of the Book of Mormon to take home and read. "He told me," Juan explains, "that the book contained the 'fulness of the gospel,' that there were promises in it concerning my forefathers, and also that it was the history of the Lamanite nation.

"Each day I thought of these things. First I wondered if the missionaries were true messengers of God—or were they de-ceivers? Second, I wondered if the book could be the truth. What was I to do? Finally, one night I sought the Lord in simple prayer, asking him to tell me if the things I had read were true and if the Book of Mormon was a book of God. At that time, I could not give an elaborate prayer—as one can pray when he has been a member of the Church for years. I asked the Lord in simplicity to help me and teach me.

"On this particular night, I had read three chapters in First Nephi. I hid the Book of Mormon among my school books, tremb-ling with fear that my parents might discover it. They were fervent Catholics."

After reading and praying, Juan retired to his bed and went to sleep. As he slept, he "experienced a strange thing—as though in vision." He says, "I saw the Book of Mormon open near the center. The printed words were resplendent in their beauty; one cannot imagine how they shone—as golden as the sun. Most surprising, I was able to read the words. They were from Mosiah 15:14-15:

> And these are they who have published peace, who have brought good tidings of good, who have published salvation; and said unto Zion: Thy God reigneth!
>
> And O how beautiful upon the mountains were their feet!

"I awakened. Anxiously I took my notebook in my hands, opened it, and wrote the words that I had read in the dream. I then returned to my bed and pondered all the things I had read and seen in my sleep.

"I cannot say when I slept again, but once again I saw the Book of Mormon open. It was more brilliant than before. This time what I read was Ether 4:15-17:

> Behold, when ye shall rend that veil of unbelief which doth cause you to remain in your awful state of wickedness, and hardness of heart, and blindness of mind, then shall the great and marvelous things which have been hid up from the foundation of the world from you—yea, when ye shall call upon the Father in my name, with a broken heart and a contrite spirit, then shall ye know that the Father hath remembered the covenant which he made unto your fathers, O house of Israel.
>
> And then shall my revelations which I have caused to be written by my servant John be unfolded in the eyes of all the people. Remember, when ye see these things, ye shall know that the time is at hand that they shall be made manifest in very deed.
>
> Therefore, when ye shall receive this record ye may know that the work of the Father has commenced upon all the face of the land.

Once again I awoke, opened my notebook and recorded the words of the dream. Then I went to sleep again.

"In the morning when I awakened, I eagerly ran to look in my notebook, anxious to see whether I had actually written the words seen in my two dreams. I was overjoyed to find that I had, and that when I compared my notebook with the same chapters and verses in my copy of the Book of Mormon, the words were the same."

His prayer answered, Juan joined the Church and began a life of dedication to the Lord's work. He married and became the father of nine children. He and his wife traveled at great sacrifice to the Mesa Temple to receive their endowments and the other blessings of the House of the Lord. Six of his older children have also been through the temple.

In 1950, Elder Soriano was called to fill a full-time mission among his own people, leaving his family to till the family farm in his absence. Two of his children have likewise filled missions, and two others plan to go soon. Brother Soriano is unfaltering in his dedication to missionary service and to the Lord's work. For the past few years, he has served as priesthood advisor on the Mission Board.

"Today," he says, "I bear testimony to the truthfulness of the gospel. With gratitude in my heart, I give thanks to my Heavenly Father that he answered my prayer, not only with words of men, but with words of the living God. Since that moment, all doubts have disappeared, and my convictions have remained until this day. And as God lives, I know my testimony is true."

This account was prepared by Beth Romney, whose husband Gordon M. Romney was formerly president of the Mexican Mission.

EILEEN DAVIES

A CATHOLIC NUN DISCOVERS
THE GOSPEL

In a private audience with the Pope, Eileen Davies asked to be released from the vows she had taken as a nun more than thirty years previously. A year later her request was granted, and she became a lay Catholic.

She took this step because of growing concern and disillusionment about doctrines and practices of her church, much of which was fostered by studies she had made in the private library of the Vatican. But still she remained close to the church she had served all her life—until one day, back in her native Wales, she learned why she had been impelled to leave the convent. She discovered the true gospel of Jesus Christ.

In her late sixties at the time of her conversion, Eileen Davies has since served a mission in Italy as well as giving devoted service in other Church callings. She is now head of the English department at the Oxford School of Language in Venice, Italy; and in her spare time she travels many miles to bear testimony to people who are studying the gospel with the help of LDS missionaries. As her immensely interesting account indicates, her depth of conviction and gratitude for the gospel is an example to Latter-day Saints everywhere.

After thirty-three years as a nun, it seemed that Eileen Davies (Sister Mary Francesca) had reached the pinnacle of success. As the English representative to the Vatican, she enjoyed esteem and responsibility. Her capabilities as a teacher and governor of over two hundred convents in Italy were well known. She enjoyed audiences with the Pope. What could possibly happen to make her break with the Roman Catholic Church and eventually embrace the restored gospel of Jesus Christ? This fascinating and true story begins in Cardiff, Wales.

Eileen Davies was born in 1901, the youngest of ten children. In accordance with the prevailing custom in devout Roman Catholic homes, one child was selected to follow the ministry. This choice fell to her older brother, Cuthbert. Before he could begin the ministry, however, Cuthbert was killed in 1917, during World War I, at Ypres, Belgium. Eileen was sixteen years old at this time, and her brother's death was the first real sorrow her heart had ever sustained. She secretly felt determined to replace her brother as the family representative to the church. However, it came as a surprise to the whole family when it was announced openly that Eileen had been selected.

Surprise turned to grief in the heart of Eileen's mother. Although Eileen was sixteen years old, she was still her mother's youngest child and, therefore, her baby. Her mother remonstrated against this selection, even saying to the Mother Superior, "Take the other children, but leave me my baby." But the Mother Superior countered by saying, "It is the baby that the Lord wants."

The apprehension of Eileen's mother persisted. Within the next few months Eileen came down with a severe illness, which persisted during the ensuing two years. Her mother gradually began to despair of her life. She reasoned that the illness must have been the judgment of a displeased God. At length, she promised to allow Eileen to enter the convent if and when she regained her health. After her lengthy convalescence, the date was set on March 25, 1921, for Eileen's entrance.

Eileen traveled north approximately 140 miles to Loughborough, Leicestershire, England. She tells her experience in her own words:

"I took a taxi to the convent, as the train was two hours late and there was no carriage to meet me. The taxi stopped outside a huge door in the middle of a very high wall. I pulled the chain that rang the bell and waited the proverbial 'eternity' for the door to open. An old Sister with a sad face like the Madonna of Sorrows appeared. My heart was thumping as she beckoned me to enter. The door closed, and the huge key was turned one, two, and three times. I felt already buried alive! Again the Sister beckoned me, and I followed her through long glass cloisters.

"The windows were covered in black net curtains, and the statues were draped in purple. It was the solemn part of Lent, and the convent was in deep mourning; that day was Maunday Thursday, the day our Divine Savior washed the feet of the apostles before the feast of the Passover. The Sisters were all in the chapel chanting the office applicable to the Holy Week. But in spite of the rigorous silence that reigned, the Mother Superior, hearing of my arrival, came out and received me with open arms. She was a cousin of my mother, and was very stout and jovial, a very wonderful woman, and a good Superior. 'Thank heaven!' I thought. 'At least there is someone here with a heart and a smile.' "

Because her family was so well known to the nuns, the usual three-day wait for inspection was waived, and she was immediately given the cap and frock of a postulant. During the six months that followed, Sister Eileen was required to learn about the vows of poverty, chastity, and obedience. She experienced some difficulty with poverty when her relatives sent her an extra pair of shoes. These could not be given away within the convent. After much thought, the problem was eventually solved when she gave them back to the wardrobe keeper. Since everything belonged in common to the order, permission had to be asked for the use of any item. Regarding chastity, the rule stated that there could be no admission of a boyfriend; one could not touch a Sister, except in a religious embrace, which was to place hands on arms and to kiss the shoulder. Two Sisters were to travel together always. All letters were to be opened and censored.

Being an inquisitive person, Sister Eileen found that her greatest problem was that of obedience. It distressed her at times not to be able to read the newspaper or to talk about things of the world. Because it seemed necessary to give her a special lesson in obedience, she was directed to drive a screw into a picture until told to stop. Then she was instructed to remove the screw and repair the hole. Such lessons taught her to adapt herself, and she gained acceptance of blind obedience.

When the six months were over, Sister Eileen was allowed to begin teaching in the school for two hours a day, during the time of her novitiate. This period of time extended into two years. She was then received by ballot into the order, clothed in the habit of a nun, and given the name of Sister Mary Francesca. In her first official position, Sister Davies was sent to the county of Sussex in England to be the head mistress of St. Joseph's convent school. She soon fell in love with the children and her work. By diligent effort and sound example, she instilled the love of school in her students. They received from her a wealth of practical experience. Due to the popularity of her teaching, the school doubled in size within four years.

Because of her outstanding success, she was transferred further north to a school located at a place known as Barton-on-Humber. Some of her students at St. Joseph's loved their teacher so much that they received permission from their parents to accompany her to the new location. Here she spent six happy years, during which time she helped get the school at Barton on its feet both financially and in terms of enrollment.

At this point she received orders for another transfer. Naturally, she was perturbed about this, but being obedient she did not question the call. She packed her belongings and once more shed tears at being separated from her beloved students.

As the train bore her south to the very bottom part of England, she pondered her next assignment. A ferry ride later, she approached Carisbrooke House on the Isle of Wight, an island in the English Channel. This was to be her new home. Carisbrooke House had been the Dower House of Carisbrooke Castle. Large grounds surrounded the house. Immediately Sister Davies' active mind began to conjure up possibilities for developing the complete student.

By now she had formulated the concept that for a full and rounded education, each student should have development of the physical, social, and intellectual person, all within a religious framework. Also, being a practical teacher, she realized that all work and no play makes a dull student. Soon the grounds around the schoolhouse began to resound to the sights and sounds of net ball, hockey, swimming, hunting, riding, and gymkhanas. Her rules called for five days of study, and weekends of organized athletics and religion. There were no long faces here. Her students adored her and followed her on every excursion whether mental or physical, it made little difference; each was a new and thrillingly different experience.

But now the international clouds of gloom were gathering. It was 1939; Hitler's blitzkrieg (lightning war) had defeated Poland. France was beseiged. Anticipating Hitler's bombs, the English moved their children away from the larger cities. Many went north to Loughborough, Leicestershire, and Sister Davies was now reassigned there. Shortly, children came from all parts of the compass to this school, even from as far away as Vienna and Poland. There were 360 evacuees and refugees ranging from two-and-a-half to eighteen years of age.

If ever a teacher had to be inspired, it was now. Sister Davies had to assume the roles of teacher, guide, guardian, confidante, nurse, mother, and father. She was all of these and more for six long war years at Loughborough. Many a night, with school lights out and with the sound of bombs exploding in the distance and their flashes lighting the sky, the children solemnly marched behind Sister Davies into the cellar, with gas masks and pillows in their arms, to spend a night of terror. It is of interest that despite the bombings not one pane of glass in the school was ever broken through bombing.

Since Sister Davies had given of herself to each student as the need and occasion demanded during the long war years, it was only natural that some of the students refused to return to their homes at the end of hostilities. Indeed, this was their home, in some cases the only one they had ever known or remembered. Consequently, some heartrending scenes transpired as parents came to reclaim their children, some of whom were loath to leave. Some of the children did not know whether their parents were still alive. In two cases, final word did not come until four years later. As it turned out, all of the children had at least one remaining parent to claim them.

The war ended in 1945. On the basis of her long and out-standing service, Sister Davies was summoned to Italy. She was to be the English representative to the Rosmenian Order in the Vatican. Her job for the next six years was to travel with the Mother-General and assist in supervising over two hundred convents. These were located throughout Italy and in parts of Switzerland. During this time she had frequent audience with the Pope. Yes, Sister Davies had come a long way, and on true merit. As we look at her at this time, we are led to inquire what could make her break with this church to which she had devoted so many years of her life.

She states that the break really started in this way: During her journeys, she saw much poverty and suffering among the people. At the same time, she was in the midst of great wealth in the church. She felt that this was incongruous and unfair. During her many years of working with the students, she had spared no effort in providing physical and spiritual welfare for her charges. It caused her great concern to be working in the midst of luxury and see suffering and want about her. She sincerely felt that greater efforts could be made by the church to have all things in common. Shortly, a new ruling by the Italian Father-General fed more fuel to the flames. It was that the Nuns of the Rosmenian Order should become more cloistered and contemplative; they were henceforth to cease going out, and they were now to withdraw from the world.

This of course meant that Sister Davies would have to terminate her works of charity on the outside, which to her was unthinkable. Added to this, she began to experience certain apprehensions and fears regarding doctrine, which resulted from studies she made within the private library of the Vatican. As a result of these studies, certain fallacies of function and organization in her church became evident to her. She felt that these did not conform scripturally to the true Church. At first these thoughts were vaguely disquieting, but with further study and prayer they grew to alarming proportions. At length, she knew that she could not continue to think these thoughts and still remain in her official capacity. She felt that the only fair thing to do would be to step down. Reaching this decision caused her great soul-searching and considerable anguish.

Sister Davies thus requested a private audience with Pope Pius XII in which she asked for dispensation (permission to be released from her vows). She would still remain a member of the church, but would try to find a place and circumstances where she could become involved in works for charity. The Pope was obviously moved, and after hearing Sister Davies, he requested her to take a year to consider this decision and not to act hastily nor terminate vows at that time. To this she agreed.

She began to have yearnings to return to England and again teach. Shortly, however, in a sudden policy reversal, the Order closed some of its schools in England. This was a great blow to her. As promised, however, she did wait out the year, and then, more resolved than ever, wired for final papal confirmation of separation from her vows. This was granted, but a note was attached requesting her to sleep on it for a month. About that she says: "I had stayed awake on it for many years. There was no need for me to prolong the agony. My decision was now irrevocable."

She decided to go to London, where she could surrender her habit (nun's clothing) at the convent. Upon her arrival, the Mother Provincial greeted her with tears streaming down her cheeks. "If you must take this step," she said, "God must have some work for you to do in the world that you could not perform in the convent."

"I felt so strange and lonely as I walked to the station, but I knew that I had a mission in life and I courageously set forth to find it," she said.

A new life now began. Eileen's main interest in life had been to work with youth and the underprivileged. It was only natural that she should again turn to such work. She obtained and furnished a large flat (apartment) which she operated as a charity lodging for poor students and itinerants. Before long, however, as she began to tally the count of articles stolen from her apartment, she learned to her sorrow that not all mankind can be blindly trusted. Even her checkbook was taken, and bogus checks in her name began to appear about town. Sister Davies was eventually forced to the conclusion that thirty-three years in the convent had left her ill-prepared for this type of service.

Returning to Italy, she attended the University of Perrugia, where she took a degree in the Italian language. She then received a fine position in Venice where, between the years of 1963 and 1966, she taught at the Oxford School of Languages. During this time, she continued to remain close to the Catholic Church as a lay member, because to the best of her knowledge that church represented the closest contact she had with God. But there were many practices in the Catholic Church with which she did not agree, and the old nagging questions still left her disturbed. She sincerely prayed for guidance, desiring to know the will of God.

It was Christmas time, 1966, and Sister Davies began to think of home. Her sister was living in Cardiff, and she decided to make a Christmas visit. This was to be only temporary, as she planned to return to Venice in January to resume her teaching. On arriving in Cardiff, her first steps took her in the direction of the particular Catholic Church where she had felt drawn to the service of God in her youth. Once inside, she prayed intently, but her prayers were unanswered. The sisters whom she greeted seemed cold towards her, and spiritually she felt arid and empty. Depressed, she left the church and crossed the city to the section of Cardiff known as Rhiwbina, with the intent of visiting her sister. The familiar landmarks loomed up one by one, but as she arrived at the street on which her sister lived, she noted a new church at the corner.

"There was nothing very extraordinary about that, as many churches were built in Cardiff, and I had never crossed the road to look at any of them. But this one was different; it drew me like a magnet, and I felt constrained to cross over and read aloud the name—'The Church of Jesus Christ of Latter-day Saints.'"

She suddenly was filled with the desire to enter to find out more. Unable to enter because the building was locked, she went to her sister's home. The impression and desire to return remained strong overnight, however, and the next day she returned and found the chapel open. She entered and asked someone if she could be shown around.

She was intrigued with the classrooms and passages, and, of all things, the gymnasium (cultural hall); next, the kitchen, gleaming and bright, in which one of the LDS sisters was working. The custodian continued the tour into the chapel. Standing there and looking about, she suddenly remembered the words, "If you must leave the convent, perhaps God has some work for you to do which you could not perform here." She was very impressed by this inner feeling. After reflecting upon it, she turned and asked if there was someone who could explain to her what the church could offer spiritually. She was taken to the branch president's office, and there she met President Lawrence I. Taylor. He received Sister Davies and explained to her the basic doctrines of the Church. In a two-hour visit, the president dwelled upon the great apostasy which had robbed the Catholic Church of the priesthood and the right of succession which they claimed.

Suddenly, a great conflict began to rage in Eileen Davies' soul, for despite differences with her church and its traditions, the sum of her life efforts strained to tell her that she had been right. Yet, somehow, the words of the gospel rang true as they fell upon her ears. The story of the restoration of the gospel in this day and age sounded remarkably proper and right. However, the ties that bound her to Catholicism were hard to break. She fought hard to justify the position of the Catholic Church, but it was no use. "I knew in my heart that what I was being taught was the truth," she says, "especially when I read, meditated upon, and prayed about the Book of Mormon."

Now, she began to realize that God was offering her a great gift, the answer to all her doubts and yearnings. The only remaining obstacle was the fear of again hurting her family who already had suffered from her leaving the convent. But she realized that it was a far worse thing to fail God, and that she would have no peace until she was baptized into the restored Church.

By now, the time had passed for her to return to Italy to teach in the University. She sealed her future by sending a telegram to Italy stating that she would not be returning to teach. This decision was largely made because, at that time, there was no branch of the Church in Italy. She therefore elected to remain in Cardiff, where she could learn and grow in the gospel.

"The Elders were wonderful, although I am sure I gave them a very hard time with so many questions. But they bore their testimonies with their eyes shining with divine light. I shall always be grateful to them for their loving patience. I shall never forget the sadness in Elder Brent Dickerson's face when he said, 'You'll be baptized on the 11th of February, won't you?'

"I replied, 'Oh dear, no! It is too soon. I want to know everything about the Church before taking such a final step.'

"He answered, 'I cannot tell you everything about the Church. You will go on learning about it all your life, but when you are baptized you will have the Holy Ghost to help you to understand.'

"So I fixed the date for a week later, February 19, 1967. Oh, how happy I was that night of my baptism! I have never experienced such joy and peace. I have always suffered from aquaphobia and have never been able to go under water, but I didn't even think of it that night. I really felt Christ calling me to come to him— not 'on the waters,' but out of the waters of baptism. I felt so clean, and I knew that the Holy Ghost really had taken up residence in my soul. There was a heavenly atmosphere in the chapel that night that not only I but many other people felt and which they have told me they will never forget."

Now came the time of learning for Sister Davies and of her throwing all of her effort into the work. She loved it. Truly, this was the answer to her problems. The great plan of salvation unfolded day by day. After six months of work, prayers, study, and participation, Sister Davies was called to be the Relief Society president of the Cardiff Branch.

It was about this time that the first "all-British" Relief Society conference was held. Sister Belle Spafford and her officers came to Great Britain from Salt Lake City in 1967, and were joined by Elders Mark E. Petersen and James A. Cullimore. The conference was held in two areas, and Sister Davies was able to meet with the sisters in the London meetings. She confesses that she experienced a union of soul and Christian affection that she had never known before. She especially noted and appreciated the messages regarding deep loyalty for family and desire for exaltation as a family unit. Her greatest joy was to mingle with the saints and to love and be loved by them. She constantly commented on how this remarkable oneness reminded her of the scriptural references concerning the early saints. "See how these Christians love one another," stated their persecutors. She enjoys quoting the parallel with the modern restored church: "By this shall all men know ye are my disciples, if ye have love one unto another." Her later trip to Salt Lake City only confirmed and heightened her already deep and poignant feelings of love for the members and the restored gospel.

Sister Davies gives daily thanks to the Lord for guiding her footsteps into truth. She says:

"Every day I am more persuaded of the truth. I thank the Almighty from the bottom of my heart for the great grace he has bestowed upon me by bringing me to the knowledge of the restored gospel. There is no greater gift on earth than the knowledge given to us in the Church of Jesus Christ. I pray that I will always be worthy of this special grace bestowed upon me. I know that this Church is the true Church of Jesus Christ. I have loved my Savior all my life—he has ever been 'my God and my all.' It is impossible that he should deceive me. I could never feel so happy and contented with anything that was not the truth. I say these words humbly in the name of Jesus Christ. Amen."

This account has been compiled from details supplied by Eileen Davies and from material written by Ray H. Barton, Jr., former president of the Southwest British Mission.